Songs of the
HIGH NORTH

FURNIVAL   LODGE

No: 2558

Songs of the
HIGH NORTH

Robert Service

A & C Black
London

Reissued 1999
by A & C Black (Publishers) Limited
35 Bedford Row, London WC1R 4JH

0-7136-5082-6

This edition first published
in Great Britain 1958
by Ernest Benn Limited

A CIP catalogue record of this book is
available from the British Library.

Printed and bound in Great Britain by
The Cromwell Press, Trowbridge,
Wiltshire.

CONTENTS

SONGS OF THE HIGH NORTH

Men of the High North

MEN of the High North, the wild sky is blazing;
　　Islands of opal float on silver seas;
Swift splendours kindle, barbaric, amazing;
　　Pale ports of amber, golden argosies.
Ringed all around us the proud peaks are glowing;
　　Fierce chiefs in council, their wigwam the sky;
Far, far below us the big Yukon flowing,
　　Like threadéd quicksilver, gleams to the eye.

Men of the High North, you who have known it;
　　You in whose hearts its splendours have abode;
Can you renounce it, can you disown it?
　　Can you forget it, its glory and its goad?
Where is the hardship, where is the pain of it?
　　Lost in the limbo of things you've forgot;
Only remain the guerdon and gain of it;
　　Zest of the foray, and God, how you fought!

You who have made good, you foreign faring;
　　You money magic to far lands has whirled;
Can you forget those days of vast daring,
　　There with your soul on Top o' the World?
Nights when no peril could keep you awake on
　　Spruce boughs you spread for your couch in the snow;

Taste all your feasts like the beans and the bacon,
  Fried at the camp-fire at forty below?

Can you remember your huskies all going,
  Barking with joy and their brushes in air;
You in your parka, glad-eyed and glowing,
  Monarch, your subjects the wolf and the bear?
Monarch, your kingdom unravisht and gleaming;
  Mountains your throne, and a river your car;
Crash of a bull moose to rouse you from dreaming;
  Forest your couch, and your candle a star.

You who this faint day the High North is luring
  Unto her vastness, taintlessly sweet;
You who are steel-braced, straight-lipped, enduring,
  Dreadless in danger and dire in defeat:
Honour the High North ever and ever,
  Whether she crown you, or whether she slay;
Suffer her fury, cherish and love her—
  He who would rule he must learn to obey.

Men of the High North, fierce mountains love you;
  Proud rivers leap when you ride on their breast.
See, the austere sky, pensive above you,
  Dons all her jewels to smile on your rest.
Children of Freedom, scornful of frontiers,
  We who are weaklings honour your worth.
Lords of the wilderness, Princes of Pioneers,
  Let's have a rouse that will ring round the earth.

The Ballad of the Northern Lights

ONE of the Down and Out—that's me. Stare at me well,
ay, stare!
Stare and shrink—say! you wouldn't think that I was a
millionaire.
Look at my face, it's crimped and gouged—one of them
death-mask things;
Don't seem the sort of man, do I, as might be the pal of
kings?
Slouching along in smelly rags, a bleary-eyed, no-good
bum;
A knight of the hollow needle, pard, spewed from the
sodden slum.
Look me all over from head to foot; how much would you
think I was worth?
A dollar? a dime? a nickel? Why, *I'm the wealthiest man on
earth.*

No, don't you think that I'm off my base. You'll sing a
different tune
If only you'll let me spin my yarn. Come over to this saloon;
Wet my throat—it's as dry as chalk, and seeing as how it's
you,
I'll tell the tale of a Northern trail, and so help me God,
it's true.
I'll tell of the howling wilderness and the haggard Arctic
heights,

Of a reckless vow that I made, and how *I staked the Northern Lights.*

Remember the year of the Big Stampede and the trail of Ninety-eight,
When the eyes of the world were turned to the North, and the hearts of men elate;
Hearts of the old dare-devil breed thrilled at the wondrous strike,
And to every man who could hold a pan came the message, "Up and hike."
Well, I was there with the best of them, and I knew I would not fail.
You wouldn't believe it to see me now; but wait till you've heard my tale.

You've read of the trail of Ninety-eight, but its woe no man may tell;
It was all of a piece and a whole yard wide, and the name of the brand was "Hell."
We heard the call and we staked our all; we were plungers playing blind,
And no man cared how his neighbour fared, and no man looked behind;
For a ruthless greed was born of need, and the weakling went to the wall,
And a curse might avail where a prayer would fail, and the gold lust crazed us all.

Bold were we, and they called us three the "Unholy Trinity";
There was Ole Olson, the Sailor Swede, and the Dago Kid and me.
We were the discards of the pack, the foreloopers of Unrest,
Reckless spirits of fierce revolt in the ferment of the West.

We were bound to win and we revelled in the hardships
    of the way.
We staked our ground and our hopes were crowned, and we
    hoisted out the pay.
We were rich in a day beyond our dreams, it was gold from
    the grass-roots down;
But we weren't used to such sudden wealth, and there was
    the siren town.
We were crude and careless frontiersmen, with much in us
    of the beast;
We could bear the famine worthily, but we lost our heads
    at the feast.
The town looked mighty bright to us, with a bunch of dust
    to spend,
And nothing was half too good them days, and every one
    was our friend.
Wining meant more than mining then, and life was a dizzy
    whirl,
Gambling and dropping chunks of gold down the neck of a
    dance-hall girl;
Till we went clean mad, it seems to me, and we squandered
    our last poke,
And we sold our claim, and we found ourselves one bitter
    morning—broke.

The Dago Kid he dreamed a dream of his mother's aunt
    who died—
In the dawn-light dim she came to him, and she stood by his
    bedside,
And she said: "Go forth to the highest North till a lonely
    trail ye find;
Follow it far and trust your star, and fortune will be kind."
But I jeered at him, and then there came the Sailor Swede
    to me,
And he said: "I dreamed of my sister's son, who croaked
    at the age of three.

From the herded dead he sneaked and said: 'Seek you an
    Arctic trail;
'Tis pale and grim by the Polar rim, but seek and ye shall
    not fail.' "
And lo! that night I too did dream of my mother's sister's
    son,
And he said to me : "By the Arctic Sea there's a treasure to
    be won.
Follow and follow a lone moose trail, till you come to a
    valley grim,
On the slope of the lonely watershed that borders the Polar
    brim."
Then I woke my pals, and soft we swore by the mystic Silver
    Flail,
'Twas the hand of Fate, and to-morrow straight we would
    see the lone moose trail.

We watched the groaning ice wrench free, crash on with a
    hollow din;
Men of the wilderness were we, freed from the taint of sin.
The mighty river snatched us up and it bore us swift along;
The days were bright, and the morning light was sweet with
    jewelled song.
We poled and lined up nameless streams, portaged o'er hill
    and plain;
We burnt our boat to save the nails, and built our boat
    again;
We guessed and groped, North, ever North, with many a
    twist and turn;
We saw ablaze in the deathless days the splendid sunsets
    burn.

O'er soundless lakes where the grayling makes a rush at the
    clumsy fly;
By bluffs so steep that the hard-hit sheep falls sheer from
    out the sky;

By lilied pools where the bull moose cools and wallows in
    huge content;
By rocky lairs where the pig-eyed bears peered at our tiny
    tent.
Through the black canyon's angry foam we hurled to
    dreamy bars,
And round in a ring the dog-nosed peaks bayed to the
    mocking stars.
Spring and summer and autumn went; the sky had a tallow
    gleam,
Yet North and ever North we pressed to the land of our
    Golden Dream.

So we came at last to a tundra vast and dark and grim and
    lone;
And there was the little lone moose trail, and we knew it
    for our own.
By muskeg hollow and nigger-head it wandered endlessly;
Sorry of heart and sore of foot, weary men were we.
The short-lived sun had a leaden glare and the darkness
    came too soon,
And stationed there with a solemn stare was the pinched,
    anaemic moon.
Silence and silvern solitude till it made you dumbly shrink,
And you thought to hear with an outward ear the things
    you thought to think.

Oh, it was wild and weird and wan, and ever in camp
    o'nights
We would watch and watch the silver dance of the mystic
    Northern Lights.
And soft they danced from the Polar sky and swept in
    primrose haze;
And swift they pranced with their silver feet, and pierced
    with a blinding blaze.

They danced a cotillion in the sky; they were rose and silver
shod;
It was not good for the eyes of man—'twas a sight for the
eyes of God.
It made us mad and strange and sad, and the gold whereof
we dreamed
Was all forgot, and our only thought was of the lights that
gleamed.
Oh, the tundra sponge it was golden brown, and some was a
bright blood-red;
And the reindeer moss gleamed here and there like the
tombstones of the dead.
And in and out and around about the little trail ran clear,
And we hated it with a deadly hate and we feared with a
deadly fear.
And the skies of night were alive with light, with a throbbing
thrilling flame;
Amber and rose and violet, opal and gold it came.
It swept the sky like a giant scythe, it quivered back to a
wedge;
Argently bright, it cleft the night with a wavy golden edge.
Pennants of silver waved and streamed, lazy banners
unfurled;
Sudden splendours of sabres gleamed, lightning javelins
were hurled.
There in our awe we crouched and saw with our wild,
uplifted eyes
Charge and retire the hosts of fire in the battlefield of the
skies.

But all things come to an end at last, and the muskeg
melted away,
And frowning down to bar our path a muddle of mountains
lay.
And a gorge sheered up in granite walls, and the moose trail
crept betwixt;

'Twas as if the earth had gaped too far and her stony jaws
  were fixt.
Then the winter fell with a sudden swoop, and the heavy
  clouds sagged low,
And earth and sky were blotted out in a whirl of driving
  snow.

We were climbing up a glacier in the neck of a mountain
  pass,
When the Dago Kid slipped down and fell into a deep
  crevasse.
When we got him out one leg hung limp, and his brow
  was wreathed with pain,
And he says: " 'Tis badly broken, boys, and I'll never walk
  again.
It's death for all if ye linger here, and that's no cursèd lie;
Go on, go on while the trail is good, and leave me down to
  die."
He raved and swore, but we tended him with our uncouth,
  clumsy care.
The camp-fire gleamed and he gazed and dreamed with a
  fixed and curious stare.
Then all at once he grabbed my gun and he put it to his
  head,
And he says: "I'll fix it for you, boys!"—them are the words
  he said.

So we sewed him up in a canvas sack and we slung him
  to a tree;
And the stars like needles stabbed our eyes, and woeful men
  were we.
And on we went on our woeful way, wrapped in a daze of
  dream,
And the Northern Lights in the crystal nights came forth
  with a mystic gleam.

They danced and they danced the devil-dance over the
 naked snow;
And soft they rolled like a tide upshoaled with a ceaseless
 ebb and flow.
They rippled green with a wondrous sheen, they fluttered
 out like a fan;
They spread with a blaze of rose-pink rays never yet seen
 of man.
They writhed like a brood of angry snakes, hissing and
 sulphur pale;
Then swift they changed to a dragon vast, lashing a cloven
 tail.
It seemed to us, as we gazed aloft with an everlasting
 stare,
The sky was a pit of bale and dread, and a monster revelled
 there.

We climbed the rise of a hog-back range that was desolate
 and drear,
When the Sailor Swede had a crazy fit, and he got to talking
 queer.
He talked of his home in Oregon and the peach-trees all in
 bloom,
And the fern head-high, and the topaz sky, and the forest's
 scented gloom.
He talked of the sins of his misspent life, and then he seemed
 to brood,
And I watched him there like a fox a hare, for I knew it
 was not good.
And sure enough in the dim dawn-light I missed him from
 the tent,
And a fresh trail broke through the crusted snow, and I
 knew not where it went.
But I followed it o'er the seamless waste, and I found him
 at shut of day,
Naked there as a new-born babe—so I left him where
 he lay.

Day after day was sinister, and I fought fierce-eyed despair,
And I clung to life, and I struggled on, I knew not why nor
where.
I packed my grub in short relays, and I cowered down in my
tent,
And the world around was purged of sound like a frozen
continent.
Day after day was dark as death, but ever and ever at nights,
With a brilliancy that grew and grew, blazed up the
Northern Lights.
They rolled around with a soundless sound like softly
bruisèd silk;
They poured into the bowl of the sky with the gentle flow
of milk.
In eager, pulsing violet their wheeling chariots came,
Or they poised above the Polar rim like a coronal of
flame.
From depths of darkness fathomless their lancing rays were
hurled,
Like the all-combining searchlights of the navies of the
world.
There on the roof-pole of the world as one bewitched I
gazed,
And howled and grovelled like a beast as the awful splen-
dours blazed.
My eyes were seared, yet thralled I peered through the parka
hood nigh blind;
But I staggered on to the lights that shone, and never I
looked behind.
There is a mountain round and low that lies by the Polar
rim,
And I climbed its height in a whirl of light, and I peered
o'er its jagged brim;
And there in a crater deep and vast, ungained, unguessed
of men.
The mystery of the Arctic world was flashed into my ken.

For there these poor dim eyes of mine beheld the sight of
sights—
That hollow ring was the source and spring of the mystic
Northern Lights.

Then I staked that place from crown to base, and I hit the
homeward trail.
Ah, God! it was good, though my eyes were blurred, and I
crawled like a sickly snail.
In that vast white world where the silent sky communes
with the silent snow,
In hunger and cold and misery I wandered to and fro.
But the Lord took pity on my pain, and He led me to the
sea,
And some ice-bound whalers heard my moan, and they fed
and sheltered me.
They fed the feeble scarecrow thing that stumbled out of
the wild
With the ravaged face of a mask of death and the wandering
wits of a child—
A craven, cowering bag of bones that once had been a man.
They tended me and they brought me back to the world,
and here I am.

Some say that the Northern Lights are the glare of the Arctic
ice and snow;
And some that it's electricity, and nobody seems to know.
But I'll tell you now—and if I lie, may my lips be stricken
dumb—
It's a *mine*, a mine of the precious stuff that men call
radium.
It's a million dollars a pound, they say, and there's tons and
tons in sight.
You can see it gleam in a golden stream in the solitudes of
night.

And it's mine, all mine—and say! if you have a hundred
plunks to spare,
I'll let you have the chance of your life, I'll sell you a quarter
share.
You turn it down? Well, I'll make it ten, seeing as you are
my friend.
Nothing doing? Say! don't be hard—have you got a dollar
to lend?
Just a dollar to help me out, I know you'll treat me
white;
I'll do as much for you some day . . . God bless you, sir;
good-night.

* * *

The Ballad of Blasphemous Bill

I TOOK a contract to bury the body of blasphemous Bill
MacKie,
Whenever, wherever, or whatsoever the manner of death he
die—
Whether he die in the light o' day or under the peak-faced
moon;
In cabin or dance-hall, camp or dive, mucklucks or patent
shoon;
On velvet tundra or virgin peak, by glacier, drift or
draw;
In muskeg hollow or canyon gloom, by avalanche, fang or
claw;
By battle, murder or sudden wealth, by pestilence, hooch or
lead—
I swore on the Book I would follow and look till I found my
tombless dead.

For Bill was a dainty kind of cuss, and his mind was mighty
    sot
On a dinky patch with flowers and grass in a civilised bone-
    yard lot.
And where he died or how he died, it didn't matter a damn
So long as he had a grave with frills and a tombstone
    "epigram."
So I promised him, and he paid the price in good cheechako
    coin
(Which the same I blowed in that very night down in the
    Tenderloin).
Then I painted a three-foot slab of pine: "Here lies poor Bill
    MacKie,"
And I hung it up on my cabin wall and I waited for Bill to
    die.

Years passed away, and at last one day came a squaw with a
    story strange,
Of a long-deserted line of traps 'way back of the Bighorn
    range;
Of a little hut by the great divide, and a white man stiff and
    still,
Lying there by his lonesome self, and I figured it must be
    Bill.
So I thought of the contract I'd made with him, and I took
    down from the shelf
The swell black box with the silver plate he'd picked out for
    himself;
And I packed it full of grub and "hooch," and I slung it on
    the sleigh;
Then I harnessed up my team of dogs and was off at dawn of
    day.

You know what it's like in the Yukon wild when it's sixty-
    nine below;

When the ice-worms wriggle their purple heads through the
    crust of the pale blue snow;
When the pine-trees crack like little guns in the silence of
    the wood,
And the icicles hang down like tusks under the parka hood;
When the stove-pipe smoke breaks sudden off, and the sky
    is weirdly lit,
And the careless feel of a bit of steel burns like a red-hot spit;
When the mercury is a frozen ball, and the frost-fiend stalks
    to kill—
Well, it was just like that that day when I set out to look for
    Bill.

Oh, the awful hush that seemed to crush me down on every
    hand,
As I blundered blind with a trail to find through that blank
    and bitter land;
Half dazed, half crazed in the winter wild, with its grim
    heart-breaking woes,
And the ruthless strife for a grip on life that only the sour-
    dough knows!
North by the compass, North I pressed; river and peak and
    plain
Passed like a dream I slept to lose and I waked to dream
    again.

River and plain and mighty peak—and who could stand
    unawed?
As their summits blazed, he could stand undazed at the foot
    of the throne of God.
North, aye, North, through a land accurst, shunned by the
    scouring brutes,
And all I heard was my own harsh word and the whine of
    the malamutes,
Till at last I came to a cabin squat, built in the side of a hill,

And I burst in the door, and there on the floor, frozen to
death, lay Bill.

Ice, white ice, like a winding-sheet, sheathing each smoke-
grimed wall;
Ice on the stove-pipe, ice on the bed, ice gleaming over all;
Sparkling ice on the dead man's chest, glittering ice in his
hair,
Ice on his fingers, ice in his heart, ice in his glassy stare;
Hard as a log and trussed like a frog, with his arms and legs
outspread.
I gazed at the coffin I'd brought for him, and I gazed at the
gruesome dead,
And at last I spoke: "Bill liked his joke; but still, goldarn
his eyes,
A man had ought to consider his mates in the way he goes
and dies."

Have you ever stood in an Arctic hut in the shadow of the
Pole,
With a little coffin six by three and a grief you can't control?
Have you ever sat by a frozen corpse that looks at you with a
grin,
And that seem to say: "You may try all day, but you'll
never jam me in?"
I'm not a man of the quitting kind, but I never felt so blue
As I sat there gazing at that stiff and studying what I'd do.
Then I rose and I kicked off the husky dogs that were nosing
round about,
And I lit a roaring fire in the stove, and I started to thaw Bill
out.

Well, I thawed and thawed for thirteen days but it didn't
seem no good;
His arms and legs stuck out like pegs, as if they was made of
wood.

Till at last I said: "It ain't no use—he's froze too hard to
  thaw;
He's obstinate, and he won't lie straight, so I guess I got to—
  saw."
So I sawed off poor Bill's arms and legs, and I laid him snug
  and straight
In the little coffin he picked hisself, with the dinky silver
  plate;
And I came nigh near to shedding a tear as I nailed him
  safely down;
Then I stowed him away in my Yukon sleigh, and I started
  back to town.

So I buried him as the contract was in a narrow grave and
  deep,
And there he's waiting the Great Clean-up, when the Judg-
  ment sluice-heads sweep;
And I smoke my pipe and I meditate in the light of the
  Midnight Sun,
And sometimes I wonder if they *was*, the awful things I
  done.
And as I sit and the parson talks, expounding of the Law,
I often think of poor old Bill—*and how hard he was to saw.*

* * *

The Man from Eldorado

I

HE'S the man from Eldorado, and he's just arrived in town,
  In moccasins and oily buckskin shirt.
He's gaunt as any Indian, and pretty nigh as brown;
  He's greasy, and he smells of sweat and dirt.

He sports a crop of whiskers that would shame a healthy
    hog;
    Hard work has racked his joints and stooped his back;
He slops along the sidewalk followed by his yellow dog,
    But he's got a bunch of gold-dust in his sack.

He seems a little wistful as he blinks at all the lights,
    And maybe he is thinking of his claim
And the dark and dwarfish cabin where he lay and dreamed
    at nights,
    (Thank God, he'll never see the place again!)
Where he lived on tinned tomatoes, beef embalmed and
    sour dough bread,
    On rusty beans and bacon furred with mould;
His stomach's out of kilter and his system full of lead,
    But it's over, and his poke is full of gold.

He has panted at the windlass, he has loaded in the drift,
    He has pounded at the face of oozy clay;
He has taxed himself to sickness, dark and damp and
    double shift,
    He has laboured like a demon night and day.
And now, praise God, it's over, and he seems to breathe
    again
    Of new-mown hay, the warm, wet, friendly loam;
He sees a snowy orchard in a green and dimpling plain,
    And a little vine-clad cottage, and it's—Home.

II

He's the man from Eldorado, and he's had a bite and sup,
    And he's met in with a drouthy friend or two;
He's cached away his gold-dust, but he's sort of bucking up,
    So he's kept enough to-night to see him through.
His eye is bright and genial, his tongue no longer lags;
    His heart is brimming o'er with joy and mirth;

He may be far from savoury, he may be clad in rags,
  But to-night he feels as if he owns the earth.

Says he: "Boys, here is where the shaggy North and I will
    shake;
  I thought I'd never manage to get free.
I kept on making misses; but at last I've got my stake;
  There's no more thawing frozen muck for me.
I am going to God's Country, where I'll live the simple life;
  I'll buy a bit of land and make a start;
I'll carve a little homestead, and I'll win a little wife,
  And raise ten little kids to cheer my heart."

They signified their sympathy by crowding to the bar;
  They bellied up three deep and drank his health.
He shed a radiant smile around and smoked a rank cigar;
  They wished him honour, happiness and wealth.
They drank unto his wife to be—that unsuspecting maid;
  They drank unto his children half a score;
And when they got through drinking, very tenderly they laid
  The man from Eldorado on the floor.

III

He's the man from Eldorado, and he's only starting in
  To cultivate a thousand-dollar jab.
His poke is full of gold-dust and his heart is full of sin,
  And he's dancing with a girl called Muckluck Mag.
She's as light as any fairy; she's as pretty as a peach;
  She's mistress of the witchcraft to beguile;
There's sunshine in her manner, there is music in her
    speech,
  And there's concentrated honey in her smile.

Oh, the fever of the dance-hall and the glitter and the shine
  The beauty, and the jewels and the whirl,

The madness of the music, the rapture of the wine,
  The languorous allurement of a girl!
She is like a lost madonna; he is gaunt, unkempt and grim;
  But she fondles him and gazes in his eyes;
Her kisses seek his heavy lips, and soon it seems to him
  He has staked a little claim in Paradise.

"Who's for a juicy two-step?" cries the master of the
      floor;
  The music throbs with soft, seductive beat.
There's glitter, gilt and gladness; there are pretty girls
      galore;
  There's a woolly man with moccasins on feet.
They know they've got him going; he is buying wine for all;
  They crowd around as buzzards at a feast,
Then when his poke is empty they boost him from the hall,
  And spurn him in the gutter like a beast.

He's the man from Eldorado, and he's painting red the
      town;
  Behind he leaves a trail of yellow dust;
In a whirl of senseless riot he is ramping up and down;
  There's nothing checks his madness and his lust.
And soon the word is passed around—it travels like a flame;
  They fight to clutch his hand and call him friend,
The chevaliers of lost repute, the dames of sorry fame;
  Then comes the grim awakening—the end.

IV

He's the man from Eldorado, and he gives a grand affair;
  There's feasting, dancing, wine without restraint.
The smooth Beau Brummels of the bar, the faro men, are
      there;
  The tinhorns and purveyors of red paint;

The sleek and painted women, their predacious eyes aglow—
  Sure Klondike City never saw the like;
Then Muckluck Mag proposed the toast, "The giver of the
    show,
  The livest sport that ever hit the pike."

The "live one" rises to his feet; he stammers to reply—
  And then there comes before his muddled brain
A vision of green vastitudes beneath an April sky,
  And clover pastures drenched with silver rain.
He knows that it can never be, that he is down and out;
  Life leers at him with foul and fetid breath;
And then amid the revelry, the song and cheer and shout,
  He suddenly grows grim and cold as death.

He grips the table tensely, and he says : "Dear friends of
    mine,
  I've let you dip your fingers in my purse;
I've crammed you at my table, and I've drowned you in my
    wine,
  And I've little left to give you but—my curse.
I've failed supremely in my plans; it's rather late to whine;
  My poke is mighty weasened up and small.
I thank you each for coming here; the happiness is mine—
  And now, you thieves and harlots, take it all."

He twists the thong from off his poke; he swings it o'er his
    head;
  The nuggets fall around their feet like grain.
They rattle over roof and wall; they scatter, roll and spread;
  The dust is like a shower of golden rain.
The guests a moment stand aghast, then grovel on the floor;
  They fight, and snarl, and claw, like beasts of prey;
And then, as everybody grabbed and everybody swore,
  The man from Eldorado slipped away.

V

He's the man from Eldorado, and they found him stiff and
    dead,
    Half covered by the freezing ooze and dirt.
A clotted Colt was in his hand, a hole was in his head,
    And he wore an old and oily buckskin shirt.
His eyes were fixed and horrible, as one who hails the end;
    The frost had set him rigid as a log;
And there, half lying on his breast, his last and only friend,
    There crouched and whined a mangy yellow dog.

*   *   *

My Friends

THE man above was a murderer, the man below was a thief;
And I lay there in the bunk between, ailing beyond belief;
A weary armful of skin and bone, wasted with pain and grief.

My feet were froze, and the lifeless toes were purple and
    green and grey;
The little flesh that clung to my bones, you could punch it in
    holes like clay;
The skin on my gums was a sullen black, and slowly peeling
    away.

I was sure enough in a direful fix, and often I wondered why
They did not take the chance that was left and leave me
    alone to die,
Or finish me off with a dose of dope—so utterly lost was I.

But no; they brewed me the green-spruce tea, and nursed
    me there like a child;

And the homicide he was good to me, and bathed my sores
    and smiled;
And the thief he starved that I might be fed, and his eyes
    were kind and mild.

Yet they were woefully wicked men, and often at night in
    pain
I heard the murderer speak of his deed and dream it over
    again;
I heard the poor thief sorrowing for the dead self he had
    slain.

I'll never forget that bitter dawn, so evil, askew and grey,
When they wrapped me round in the skins of beasts and they
    bore me to a sleigh,
And we started out with the nearest post an hundred miles
    away.

I'll never forget the trail they broke, with its tense, un-
    utterable woe;
And the crunch, crunch, crunch, as their snow-shoes sank
    through the crust of the hollow snow;
And my breath would fail, and every beat of my heart was
    like a blow.

And oftentimes I would die the death, yet wake up to life
    anew;
The sun would be all ablaze on the waste, and the sky a
    blighting blue.
And the tears would rise in my snow-blind eyes and furrow
    my cheeks like dew.

And the camps we made when their strength outplayed and
    the day was pinched and wan;
And oh, the joy of that blessed halt, and how I did dread the
    dawn;

And how I hated the weary men who rose and dragged me
    on.

And oh, how I begged to rest, to rest—the snow was so
    sweet a shroud;
And oh, how I cried when they urged me on, cried and
    cursed them aloud;
Yet on they strained, all racked and pained, and sorely their
    backs were bowed.

And then it was like a lurid dream, and I prayed for a swift
    release.
From the ruthless ones who would not leave me to die alone
    in peace;
Till I wakened up and I found myself at the post of the
    Mounted Police.

And there was my friend the murderer, and there was my
    friend the thief,
With bracelets of steel around their wrists, and wicked
    beyond belief:
But when they come to God's judgment seat—may I be
    allowed the brief.

*   *   *

Clancy of the Mounted Police

IN the little Crimson Manual it's written plain and clear
That who would wear the scarlet coat shall say goodbye to
    fear;
Shall be a guardian of the right, a sleuth-hound of the trail—

In the little Crimson Manual there's no such word as
   "fail"—
Shall follow on though heavens fall, or hell's top-turrets
   freeze,
Half round the world, if need there be, on bleeding hands
   and knees.
It's duty, duty, first and last, the Crimson Manual saith;
The Scarlet Rider makes reply: "It's duty—to the death."
And so they sweep the solitudes, free men from all the earth;
And so they sentinel the woods, the wilds that know their
   worth;
And so they scour the startled plains and mock at hurt and
   pain,
And read their Crimson Manual, and find their duty plain.
Knights of the lists of unrenown, born of the frontier's need,
Disdainful of the spoken word, exultant in the deed;
Unconscious heroes of the waste, proud players of the game,
Props of the power behind the throne, upholders of the
   name;
For thus the Great White Chief hath said, "In all my lands
   be peace,"
And to maintain his word he gave his West the Scarlet
   Police.

Livid-lipped was the valley, still as the grave of God;
   Misty shadows of mountain thinned into mists of cloud;
Corpselike and stark was the land, with a quiet that crushed
   and awed,
   And the stars of the weird sub-arctic glimmered over its
   shroud.

Deep in the trench of the valley two men stationed the Post,
   Seymour and Clancy the reckless, fresh from the long
   patrol,
Seymour, the sergeant, and Clancy—Clancy who made his
   boast

He could cinch like a bronco the Northland, and cling to
the prongs of the Pole.

Two lone men on detachment, standing for law on the trail;
Undismayed in the vastness, wise with the wisdom of
old—
Out of the night hailed a half-breed telling a pitiful tale,
"White man starving and crazy on the banks of the
Nordenscold."

Up sprang the red-haired Clancy, lean and eager of eye;
Loaded the long toboggan, strapped each dog at its post;
Whirled his lash at the leader; then, with a whoop and a cry,
Into the Great White silence faded away like a ghost.

The clouds were a misty shadow, the hills were a shadowy
mist;
Sunless, voiceless and pulseless, the day was a dream of
woe;
Through the ice-rifts the river smoked and bubbled and
hissed;
Behind was a trail fresh broken, in front the untrodden
snow.

Ahead of the dogs ploughed Clancy, haloed by streaming
breath;
Through peril of open water, through ache of insensate
cold;
Up rivers wantonly winding in a land affianced to death,
Till he came to a cowering cabin on the banks of the
Nordenscold.

Then Clancy loosed his revolver, and he strode through the
open door;
And there was the man he sought for, crouching beside
the fire;

The hair of his beard was singeing, the frost on his back was
hoar,
  And ever he crooned and chanted as if he never would
  tire:—

*"I panned and I panned in the shiny sand, and I sniped on the
river bar:*
*But I know, I know, that it's down below that the golden
treasures are:*
*So I'll wait and wait till the floods abate, and I'll sink a shaft
once more,*
*And I'd like to bet that I'll go home yet with a brass band
playing before."*

He was nigh as thin as a sliver, and he whined like a
Moosehide cur;
  So Clancy clothed him and nursed him as a mother nurses
  a child;
Lifted him on the toboggan, wrapped him in robes of fur,
  Then with the dogs sore straining started to face the wild.

Said the Wild, "I will crush this Clancy, so fearless and
insolent;
  For him will I loose my fury, and bland and buffet and
  beat;
Pile up my snows to stay him; then when his strength is
spent,
  Leap on him from my ambush and crush him under my
  feet.

"Him will I ring with my silence, compass him with my
cold;
  Closer and closer clutch him unto mine icy breast;
Buffet him with my blizzards, deep in my snows enfold,
  Claiming his life as my tribute, giving my wolves the
  rest."

Clancy crawled through the vastness; o'er him the hate of
    the Wild;
    Full on his face fell the blizzard; cheering his huskies he
        ran;
Fighting, fierce-hearted and tireless, snows that drifted and
    . piled,
    With ever and ever behind him singing the crazy man.

> *"Sing hey, sing ho, for the ice and snow,*
>   *And a heart that's ever merry:*
> *Let us trim and square with a lover's care*
>   *(For why should a man be sorry?)*
> *A grave deep, deep, with the moon a-peep,*
>   *A grave in the frozen mould.*
> *Sing hey, sing ho, for the winds that blow,*
> *And a grave deep down in the ice and snow,*
>   *A grave in the land of gold."*

Day after day of darkness, the whirl of the seething snows;
    Day after day of blindness, the swoop of the stinging
        blast;
On through a blur of fury the swing of staggering blows;
    On through a world of turmoil, empty, inane and vast.

Night with its writhing storm-whirl, night despairingly
        black;
    Night with its hours of terror, numb and endlessly long;
Night with its weary waiting, fighting the shadows back,
    And ever the crouching madman singing his crazy song.

Cold with its creeping terror, cold with its sudden clinch;
    Cold so utter you wonder if 'twill ever again be warm;
Clancy grinned as he shuddered, "Surely it isn't a cinch
    Being wet-nurse to a looney in the teeth of a Arctic
    storm."

The blizzard passed and the dawn broke, knife-edged and
    crystal clear;
    The sky was a blue-domed iceberg, sunshine outlawed
      away;
Ever by snowslide and ice-rip haunted and hovered the
    Fear;
    Ever the Wild malignant poised and panted to slay.

The lead-dog freezes in harness—cut him out of the team!
    The lung of the wheel-dog's bleeding—shoot him and let
      him lie!
On and on with the others—lash them until they scream!
    "Pull for your lives, you devils! On! To halt is to die."

There in the frozen vastness Clancy fought with his foes;
    The ache of the stiffened fingers, the cut of the snowshoe
      thong;
Cheeks black-raw through the hood-flap, eyes that tingled
    and closed,
    And ever to urge and cheer him quavered the madman's
      song.

Colder it grew and colder, till the last heat left the earth,
    And there in the great stark stillness the bale fires glinted
      and gleamed,
And the Wild all around exulted and shook with a devilish
    mirth,
    And life was far and forgotten, the ghost of a joy once
      dreamed.

Death! And one who defied it, a man of the Mounted
    Police;
    Fought it there to a standstill long after hope was gone;
Grinned through his bitter anguish, fought without let or
    cease,
    Suffering, straining, striving, stumbling, struggling on.

Till the dogs lay down in their traces, and rose and staggered
   and fell;
   Till the eyes of him dimmed with shadows, and the trail
   was so hard to see;
Till the Wild howled out triumphant, and the world was a
   frozen hell—
   Then said Constable Clancy : "I guess that it's up to me."

Far down the trail they saw him, and his hands they were
   blanched like bone;
   His face was a blackened horror, from his eyelids the salt
   rheum ran;
His feet he was lifting strangely, as if they were made of
   stone,
   But safe in his arms and sleeping he carried the crazy man.

So Clancy got into Barracks, and the boys made rather a
   scene;
   And the O.C. called him a hero, and was nice as a man
   could be;
But Clancy gazed down his trousers at the place where his
   toes had been,
   And then he howled like a husky, and sang in a shaky
   key :—

"When I go back to the old love that's true to the finger-tips,
I'll say: 'Here's bushels of gold, love,' and I'll kiss my girl
   on the lips;
'It's yours to have and to hold, love.' It's the proud, proud
   boy I'll be,
When I go back to the old love that's waited so long for me."

Lost

"Black is the sky, but the land is white—
  (O the wind, the snow and the storm!)—
Father, where is our boy tonight?
  Pray to God he is safe and warm."

"Mother, mother, why should you fear
  Safe is he, and the Arctic moon
Over his cabin shines so clear—
  Rest and sleep, 'twill be morning soon."

"It's getting dark awful sudden. Say, this is mighty queer!
  Where in the world have I got to? It's still and black as
  a tomb.
I reckoned the camp was yonder, I figured the trail was
  here—
  Nothing! Just draw and valley packed with quiet and
  gloom;
Snow that comes down like feathers, thick and gobby and
  grey;
Night that looks spiteful ugly—seems that I've lost my way.

"The cold's got an edge like a jack-knife—it must be forty
  below;
Leastways that's what it seems like—it cuts so fierce to the
  bone.
The wind's getting real ferocious; it's heaving and whirling
  the snow;
  It shrieks with a howl of fury, it dies away to a moan;

Its arms sweep round like a banshee's, swift and icily white,
And buffet and blind and beat me. Lord! it's a hell of a
    night.

"I'm all tangled up in a blizzard. There's only one thing
    to do—
    Keep on moving and moving; it's death, it's death if I rest.
Oh, God! if I see the morning, if only I struggle through,
    I'll say the prayers I've forgotten since I lay on my
    mother's breast.
I seem going round in a circle; maybe the camp is near.
    Say! did somebody holler? Was it a light I saw?
Or was it only a notion? I'll shout, and maybe they'll hear—
    No! the wind only drowns me—shout till my throat is
    raw.

"The boys are all round the camp-fire wondering when I'll
    be back.
    They'll soon be starting to seek me; they'll scarcely wait
    for the light.
What will they find, I wonder, when they come to the end of
    my track—
    A hand stuck out of a snowdrift, frozen and stiff and
    white.
That's what they'll strike, I reckon; that's how they'll find
    their pard,
    A pie-faced corpse in a snowbank—curse you, don't be a
    fool!
Play the game to the finish; bet on your very last card;
    Nerve yourself for the struggle. Oh, you coward, keep
    cool!

"I'm going to lick this blizzard; I'm going to live the night.
    It can't down me with its bluster—I'm not the kind to be
    beat.

On hands and knees will I buck it; with every breath will I
    fight;
  It's life, it's life that I fight for—never it seemed so sweet.
I know that my face is frozen; my hands are numblike and
    dead;
  But oh, my feet keep a-moving, heavy and hard and slow;
They're trying to kill me, kill me, the night that's black
    overhead,
  The wind that cuts like a razor, the whipcord lash of the
    snow.

Keep a-moving, a-moving; don't, don't stumble, you fool!
  Curse this snow that's a-piling a-purpose to block my way.
It's heavy as gold in the rocker, it's white and fleecy as
    wool;
  It's soft as a bed of feathers, it's warm as a stack of hay.
Curse on my feet that slip so, my poor tired, stumbling
    feet—
  I guess they're a job for the surgeon, they feel so queerlike
    to lift—
I'll rest them just for a moment—oh, but to rest is sweet!
  The awful wind cannot get me, deep, deep down in the
    drift."

    "Father, a bitter cry I heard,
      Out of the night so dark and wild.
    Why is my heart so strangely stirred?
      'Twas like the voice of our erring child."

    "Mother, mother, you only heard
      A waterfowl in the locked lagoon—
    Out of the night a wounded bird—
      Rest and sleep, 'twill be morning soon."

Who is it talks of sleeping? I'll swear that somebody shook
  Me hard by the arm for a moment, but how on earth
    could it be?

See how my feet are moving—awfully funny they look—
   Moving as if they belonged to a some one that wasn't me.
The wind down the night's long alley bowls me down like a
     pin;
   I stagger and fall and stagger, crawl arm-deep in the snow.
Beaten back to my corner, how can I hope to win?
   And there is the blizzard waiting to give me the knockout
     blow.

Oh, I'm so warm and sleepy! No more hunger and pain.
   Just to rest for a moment; was ever rest such a joy?
Ha! what was that? I'll swear it, somebody shook me again;
   Somebody seemed to whisper: "Fight to the last, my
     boy."
Fight! That's right, I must struggle. I know that to rest
   means death;

     .   .   .   .   .

   Death, but then what does death mean?—ease from a
     world of strife.
Life has been none too pleasant; yet with my failing breath
   Still and still must I struggle, fight for the gift of life.

     .   .   .   .   .

Seems that I must be dreaming! Here is the old home trail!
   Yonder a light is gleaming; oh, I know it so well!
The air is scented with clover; the cattle wait by the rail;
   Father is through with the milking; there goes the supper-
     bell.

     .   .   .   .   .

Mother, your boy is crying, out in the night and cold;
   Let me in and forgive me, I'll never be bad any more:
I'm, oh, so sick and so sorry; please, dear mother, don't
   scold—
   It's just your boy, and he wants you . . . Mother, open
     the door. . . .

"Father, father, I saw a face
  Pressed just now to the window-pane!
Oh, it gazed for a moment's space,
  Wild and wan, and was gone again!"
"Mother, mother, you saw the snow
  Drifted down from the maple-tree
(Oh, the wind that is sobbing so!
  Weary and worn and old are we)—
Only the snow and a wounded loon—
  Rest and sleep, 'twill be morning soon."

*   *   *

The Gramophone at Fond-du-lac

Now Eddie Malone got a swell grammyfone, to draw all the
    trade to his store;
An' sez he : "Come along for a season of song, which the like
    ye had niver before."
Then Dogrib an' Slave, an' Yellow-knife brave, an' Cree in
    his dinky canoe,
Confluated near, to see an' to hear Ed's grammyfone make
    its dayboo.

Then Ed turned the crank, an' there on the bank they
    squatted like bumps on a log,
For acres around there wasn't a sound, not even the howl of
    a dog.
When out of the horn there sudden was born such a marvel-
    lous elegant tone;
An' then like a spell on that auddyence fell the voice of its
    first grammyfone.

"*Bad medicine!*" cried Old Tom, the One-eyed, an' made for
    to jump in the lake;
But no one gave heed to his little stampede, so he guessed
    he had made a mistake.
Then Roll-in-the-Mud, a chief of the blood, observed in
    choice Chippewayan:
"You've brought us canned beef, an' it's now my belief,
    that this here's a case of '*canned man*.' "

Well, though I'm not strong on the Dago in song, that sure
    got me goin' for fair.
There was Crusoe an' Scotty an' Ma'am Shoeman, Hank,
    an' Melber an' Bonchy was there.
'Twas silver an' gold, an' sweetness untold, to hear all them
    big guinneys sing;
An' thick all around an' inhalin' the sound, them Indians
    formed in a ring.

So solemn they sat, an' they smoked an' they spat, but their
    eyes sort o' glistened an' shone:
Yet niver a word of approvin' occurred till that guy Harry
    Lauder came on.
Then hunter of moose an' squaw an' papoose jest laughed
    till their stummicks was sore;
Six times Eddie set back that record an' yet they hollered an'
    hollered for more.

I'll never forget that frame-up, you bet; them caverns of
    sunset agleam;
Them still peaks aglow, them shadders below, an' the lake
    like a petrified dream;
The teepees that stood by the edge of the wood; the evenin'
    star blinkin' alone;
The peace an' the rest, an' final an' best, the music of Ed's
    grammyfone.

Then sudden an' clear there rang on my ear a song mighty
    simple an' old;
Heart-hungry an' high it thrilled to the sky, all about "silver
    threads in the gold."
'Twas tender to tears, an' it brung back the years, the
    mem'ries that hallow an' yearn;
'Twas home-love an' joy, 'twas the thought of my boy . . .
    an' right there I vowed I'd return.

Big Four-finger Jack was right at my back, an' I saw with a
    kind o' surprise,
He gazed at the lake with a heartful of ache, an' the tears
    irrigated his eyes.
An' sez he: "Cuss me, pard! but that there hits me hard;
    I've a mother does nuthin' but wait;
She's turned eighty-three, an' she's only got me, an' I'm
    scared it'll soon be too late."

      .   .   .   .   .

On Fond-du-lac's shore I'm hearin' once more that blessed
    old grammyfone play.
The summer's all gone, an' I'm still livin' on in the same old
    haphazardous way.
Oh, I cut out the booze, an' with muscles an' thews I
    corralled all the coin to go back;
But it wasn't to be—he'd a mother, you see—so I—*slipped it
    to Four-finger Jack.*

The Land of Beyond

HAVE ever you heard of the Land of Beyond,
  That dreams at the gates of the day?
Alluring it lies at the skirts of the skies,
  And ever so far away;
Alluring its calls: O ye the yoke galls,
  And ye of the trail overfond,
With saddle and pack, by paddle and track,
  Let's go to the Land of Beyond!

Have ever you stood where the silences brood,
  And vast the horizons begin,
At the dawn of the day to behold far away
  The goal you would strive for and win?
Yet, ah! in the night when you gain to the height,
  With the vast pool of heaven star-spawned,
Afar and agleam, like a valley of dream,
  Still mocks you a Land of Beyond.

Thank God! there is always a Land of Beyond
  For us who are true to the trail;
A vision to seek, a beckoning peak,
  A farness that never will fail;
A pride in our soul that mocks at a goal,
  A manhood that irks at a bond,
And try how we will, unattainable still,
  Beyond it, our Land of Beyond.

Athabaska Dick

WHEN the boys come out from Lac Labiche in the lure of
the early Spring,
  To take the pay of the "Hudson's Bay," as their fathers
  did before,
They are all aglee for the jamboree, and they make the
Landing ring
  With a whoop and a whirl, and a "Grab your girl," and a
  rip and a skip and a roar.
For the spree of Spring is a sacred thing, and the boys must
have their fun;
  Packer and tracker and half-breed Cree, from the boat to
  the bar they leap;
And then when the long flotilla goes, and the last of their
pay is done,
  The boys from the bank of Lac Labiche swing to the
  heavy sweep.
And oh, how they sigh! and their throats are dry, and sorry
are they and sick:
Yet there's none so cursed with a lime-kiln thirst as that
Athabaska Dick.

He was long and slim and lean of limb, but strong as a
stripling bear;
  And by the right of his skill and might he guided the Long
  Brigade.
All water-wise were his laughing eyes, and he steered with a
careless care,

And he shunned the shock of foam and rock, till they
    came to the Big Cascade.
And here they must make the long *portage*, and the boys
    sweat in the sun;
    And they heft and pack, and they haul and track, and each
      must do his trick;
But their thoughts are far in the Landing bar, where the
    founts of nectar run:
    And no man thinks of such gorgeous drinks as that Atha-
      baska Dick.

'Twas the close of day, and his long boat lay just over the
    Big Cascade,
    When there came to him one Jack-pot Jim, with a wild
      light in his eye;
And he softly laughed, and he led Dick aft, all eager, yet
    half afraid,
    And snugly stowed in his coat he showed a pilfered flask
      of "rye."
And in haste he slipped, or in fear he tripped, but—Dick in
    warning roared—
    And there rang a yell, and it befell that Jim was overboard.
Oh, I heard a splash, and quick as a flash I knew he could
    not swim.
    I saw him whirl in the river swirl, and thresh his arms
      about.
In a queer, strained way I heard Dick say : "I'm going after
    him,"
    Throw off his coat, leap down the boat—and then I gave
      a shout:
"Boys, grab him, quick! You're crazy, Dick : Far better
    one than two!
    Hell, man! You know you've got no show! It's sure and
      certain death . . ."
And there we hung, and there we clung, with beef and
    brawn and thew,

And sinews cracked and joints were racked, and panting
    came our breath;
And there we swayed and there we prayed, still strength and
    hope were spent—
Then Dick, he threw us off like rats and after Jim he went.

With a mighty urge amid the surge of river-rage he leapt,
    And gripped his mate and desperate he fought to gain the
    shore;
With teeth agleam he bucked the stream, yet swift and sure
    he swept
    To meet the mighty cataract that waited all aroar.
And there we stood like carven wood, our faces sickly white,
    And watched him as he beat the foam, and inch by inch
    he lost;
And nearer, nearer drew the fall, and fiercer grew the fight,
    Till on the very cascade crest a last farewell he tossed.
Then down and down and down they plunged into that pit
    of dread;
And mad we tore along the shore to claim our bitter dead.

And from that hell of frenzied foam, that crashed and fumed
    and boiled,
    Two little bodies bubbled up, and they were heedless
    then;
And oh, they lay like senseless clay! and bitter hard we
    toiled,
    Yet never, never gleam of hope, and we were weary men.
And moments mounted into hours, and black was our
    despair;
    And faint were we, and we were fain to give them up as
    dead,
When suddenly I thrilled with hope : "Back, boys! and give
    him air;
    I feel the flutter of his heart . . ." And, as the word I said,

Dick gave a sigh, and gazed around, and saw our breathless
  band;
  And saw the sky's blue floor above, all strewn with golden
    fleece;
And saw his comrade Jack-pot Jim, and touched him with
  his hand;
  And then there came into his eyes a look of perfect peace.
And as there, at his very feet, the thwarted river raved,
I heard him murmur low and deep: "Thank God! the
  whiskey's saved."

*   *   *

The Nostomaniac

On the ragged edge of the world I'll roam,
And the home of the wolf shall be my home,
And a bunch of bones on the boundless snows
The end of my trail . . . who knows, who knows!

I'm dreaming to-night in the fire-glow, alone in my study
  tower,
  My books battalioned around me, my Kipling flat on my
    knee;
But I'm not in the mood for reading, I haven't moved for
  an hour;
  Body and brain I'm weary, weary the heart of me;
Weary of crushing a longing it's little I understand,
  For I thought that my trail was ended, I thought I had
    earned my rest;
But oh, it's stronger than life is, the call of the heartless land!
  And I turn to the North in my trouble, as a child to the
    mother-breast.

Here in my den it's quiet; the sea-wind taps on the pane;
　　There's comfort and ease and plenty, the smile of the
　　　　South is sweet.
All that a man might long for, fight for and seek in vain,
　　Pictures and books and music, pleasure my last retreat.
Peace! I thought I had gained it, I swore that my tale was
　　told;
By my hair that is grey I swore it, by my eyes that are slow
　　to see;
Yet what does it all avail me? to-night, to-night, as of old,
　　Out of the dark I hear it—the Northland calling to me.

And I'm daring a rampageous river that runs the devil
　　knows where;
My hand is a-thrill on the paddle, the birch-bark bounds
　　like a bird.
Hark to the rumble of rapids! Here in my morris chair,
　　Eager and tense I'm straining—isn't it most absurd?
Now in the churn and the lather, foam that hisses and stings,
　　Leap I, keyed for the struggle, fury and fume and roar;
Rocks are spitting like hell-cats—Oh, it's a sport for kings,
　　Life on a twist of the paddle . . . there's my "Kim" on the
　　　　floor.

How I thrill and I vision! Then my camp of a night;
　　Red and gold of the fire-glow, net afloat in the stream;
Scent of the pines and silence, little "pal" pipe alight,
　　Body a-purr with pleasure, sleep untroubled of dream:
Banquet of paystreak bacon! moment of joy divine,
　　When the bannock is hot and gluey, and the teapot's
　　　　nearing the boil!
Never was wolf so hungry, stomach cleaving to spine . . .
　　Ha! there's my servant calling, says that dinner will spoil.

What do I want with dinner? Can I eat any more?
　　Can I sleep as I used to? . . . Oh, I abhor this life!

Give me the Great Uncertain, the Barren Land for a floor,
  The Milky Way for a roof-beam, splendour and space and
    strife:
Something to fight and die for—the limpid Lake of the Bear,
  The Empire of Empty Bellies, the dunes where the
    Dogribs dwell;
Big things, real things, live things . . . here in my morris
    chair,
  How I ache for the Northland! "Dinner and servants"—
    Hell!

Am I too old, I wonder? Can I take one trip more?
  Go to the granite-ribbed valleys, flooded with sunset
    wine,
Peaks that pierce the aurora, rivers I must explore,
  Lakes of a thousand islands, millioning hordes of the
    Pine?
Do they miss me, I wonder, valley and peak and plain?
  Whispering each to the other: "Many a moon has
    passed . . .
Where has he gone, our lover? Will he come back again?
  Star with his fires our tundra, leave us his bones at last?"

Yes, I'll go back to the Northland, back to the way of the
    bear,
  Back to the muskeg and mountain, back to the ice-
    leaguered sea.
Old am I! What does it matter? Nothing I would not dare;
  Give me a trail to conquer—Oh, it is "meat" to me!
I will go back to the Northland, feeble and blind and lame;
  Sup with the sunny-eyed Husky, eat moose-nose with the
    Cree;
Play with the Yellow-knife bastards, boasting my blood and
    my name:
  I will go back to the Northland, for the Northland is
    calling to me.

Then give to me paddle and whiplash, and give to me
 tumpline and gun;
 Give to me salt and tobacco, flour and a gunny of tea;
Take me up over the Circle, under the flamboyant sun;
 Turn me foot-loose like a savage—that is the finish of me.
I know the trail I am seeking, it's up by the Lake of the Bear;
 It's down by the Arctic Barrens, it's over to Hudson's
 Bay;
Maybe I'll get there—maybe: death is set by a hair . . .
 Hark! it's the Northland calling! now must I go away . . .

  Go to the Wild that waits for me;
  Go where the moose and the musk-ox be;
  Go to the wolf and the secret snows;
  Go to my fate . . . who knows, who knows!

✱ ✱ ✱

The Atavist

WHAT are you doing here, Tom Thorne, on the white
 top-knot of the world,
 Where the wind has the cut of a naked knife and the stars
 are rapier keen?
Hugging a smudgy willow fire, deep in a lynx robe curled;
 You that's a lord's own son, Tom Thorne—what does
 your madness mean?

Go home, go home to your clubs, Tom Thorne! home to
 your evening dress!
 Home to your place of power and pride, and the feast
 that waits for you!

Why do you linger all alone in the splendid emptiness,
  Scouring the Land of the Little Sticks on the trail of the
    caribou?

Why did you fall off the Earth, Tom Thorne, out of our
    social ken?
  What did your deep damnation prove? What was your
    dark despair?
Oh, with the width of a world between, and years to the
    count of ten,
  If they cut out your heart to-night, Tom Thorne, *her*
    name would be graven there.

And you fled afar for the thing called Peace, and you thought
    you would find it here,
  In the purple tundras vastly spread, and the mountains
    whitely piled;
It's a weary quest and a dreary quest, but I think that the
    end is near;
  For they say that the Lord has hidden it in the secret heart
    of the Wild.

And you know that heart as few men know, and your eyes
    are fey and deep,
  With a "something lost" come welling back from the raw,
    red dawn of life:
With woe and pain have you greatly lain, till out of abysmal
    sleep
  The soul of the Stone Age leaps in you, alert for the
    ancient strife.

And if you came to our feast again, with its pomp and glee
    and glow,
  I think you would sit stone-still, Tom Thorne, and see in
    a daze of dream

A mad sun goading to frenzied flame the glittering gems of
  the snow,
  And a monster musk-ox bulking black against the blood-
  red gleam.

I think you would see berg-battling shores, and stammer and
  halt and stare
  With a sudden sense of the frozen void, serene and vast
  and still;
And the aching gleam and the hush of dream, and the track
  of a great white bear,
  And the primal lust that surged in you as you sprang to
  make your kill.

I think you would hear the bull-moose call, and the glutted
  river roar,
  And spy the hosts of the caribou shadow the shining
  plain;
And feel the pulse of the silences, and stand elate once more
  On the verge of the yawning vastitudes that call to you in
  vain.

For I think you are one with the stars and the sun, and the
  wind and the wave and the dew;
  And the peaks untrod that yearn to God and the valleys
  undefiled;
Men soar with wings, and they bridle kings, but what is it all
  to you,
  Wise in the ways of the wilderness, and strong with the
  strength of the Wild?

You have spent your life, you have waged your strife where
  never we play a part;
  You have held the throne of the Great Unknown, you
  have ruled a kingdom vast:

.   .   .   .   .

But to-night there's a strange, new trail for you, and you go,
O weary heart!
To the peace and rest of the Great Unguessed . . . at last,
Tom Thorne, at last.

*   *   *

Barb-wire Bill

AT dawn of day the white land lay all gruesome-like and
grim,
When Bill McGee he says to me: "We've *got* to do it, Jim.
We've got to make Fort Liard quick. I know the river's bad,
But, oh! the little woman's sick . . . why! don't you savvy,
lad?"
And me! Well, yes, I must confess it wasn't hard to see
Their little family group of two would soon be one of three.
And so I answered, careless-like: "Why, Bill! you don't
suppose
I'm scared of that there 'babbling brook'? Whatever you say
—goes."

A real live man was Barb-wire Bill, with insides copper-lined;
For "barb-wire" was the brand of "hooch" to which he
most inclined.
They knew him far; his igloos are on Kittiegazuit strand.
They knew him well, the tribes who dwell within the Barren
Land.
From Koyokuk to Kuskoquim his fame was everywhere;
And he did love, all life above, that little Julie Claire,
The lithe, white slave-girl he had bought for seven hundred
skins.
And taken to his wickiup to make his moccasins.

We crawled down to the river bank, and feeble folk were we,
That Julie Claire from God-knows-where, and Barb-wire
Bill and me.
From shore to shore we heard the roar the heaving ice-floes
make,
And loud we laughed, and launched our raft, and followed in
their wake.
The river swept and seethed and leapt, and caught us in its
stride;
And on we hurled amid a world that crashed on every side.
With sullen din the banks caved in; the shore-ice lanced the
stream;
The naked floes like spooke arose, all jigging and agleam.
Black anchor-ice of strange device shot upward from its bed,
As night and day we cleft our way, and arrow-like we sped.

But "Faster still!" cried Barb-wire Bill, and looked the live-
long day
In dull despair at Julie Claire, where white like death she lay,
And sometimes he would seem to pray and sometimes seem
to curse,
And bent above with eyes of love, yet ever she grew worse.
And as we plunged and leapt and lunged, her face was
plucked with pain,
And I could feel his nerves of steel a-quiver at the strain.
And in the night he gripped me tight as I lay fast asleep;
"The river's kicking like a steer . . . run out the forward
sweep!
That's Hell-gate Canyon right ahead; I know of old its roar,
And . . . I'll be damned! *the ice is jammed!* We've got to
make the shore."

With one wild leap I gripped the sweep. The night was black
as sin.
The float-ice crashed and ripped and smashed, and stunned
us with its din.

And near and near, and clear and clear I heard the canyon
    boom;
And swift and strong we swept along to meet our awful
    doom.
And as with dread I glimpsed ahead the death that waited
    there,
My only thought was of the girl, the little Julie Claire;
And so, like demon mad with fear, I panted at the oar,
And foot by foot, and inch by inch, we worked the raft
    ashore.

The bank was staked with grinding ice, and as we scraped
    and crashed,
I only knew one thing to do, and through my mind it
    flashed:
Yet while I groped to find the rope, I heard Bill's savage cry:
"That's my job, lad! It's me that jumps. I'll snub this raft or
    die!"
I saw him leap, I saw him creep, I saw him gain the land;
I saw him crawl, I saw him fall, then run with rope in hand.
And then the darkness gulped him up, and down we dashed
    once more,

And nearer, nearer drew the jam, and thunder-like its roar.
Oh, God! all's lost . . . from Julie Claire there came a wail of
    pain,
And then—the rope grew sudden taut, and quivered at the
    strain;
It slacked and slipped, it whined and gripped, and oh, I held
    my breath!
And there we hung and there we swung right in the jaws of
    death.

A little strand of hempen rope, and how I watched it there,
With all around a hell of sound, and darkness and despair;

A little strand of hempen rope, I watched it all alone,
And somewhere in the dark behind I heard a woman moan;
And somewhere in the dark ahead I heard a man cry out,
Then silence, silence, silence fell, and mocked my hollow
     shout.
And yet once more from out the shore I heard that cry of
     pain,
A moan of mortal agony, then all was still again.

That night was hell with all the frills, and when the dawn
     broke dim,
I saw a lean and level land, but never sign of him,
I saw a flat and frozen shore of hideous device,
I saw a long-drawn strand of rope that vanished through the
     ice.
And on that treeless, rockless shore I found my partner—
     dead.
No place was there to snub the raft, so—*he had served
     instead!*

And with the rope lashed round his waist, in last defiant
     fight,
He'd thrown himself beneath the ice, that closed and gripped
     him tight;
And there he'd held us back from death, as fast in death he
     lay . . .
Say, boy! I'm not the pious brand, but—I just tried to pray.

And then I looked to Julie Clare, and sore abashed was I,
For from the robes that covered her *I heard a baby cry.* . . .

.   .   .   .   .

Thus was Love conqueror of death, and life for life was given;
And though no saint on earth, d'ye think Bill's squared hisself
     with Heaven?

Death in the Arctic

I

I TOOK the clock down from the shelf;
"At eight," said I, "I shoot myself,"
It lacked a *minute* of the hour,
And as I waited all a-cower,
A skinful of black, boding pain,
Bits of my life came back again. . . .

"Mother, there's nothing more to eat—
Why don't you go out on the street?
Always you sit and cry and cry;
Here at my play I wonder why.
Mother, when you dress up at night,
Red are your cheeks, your eyes are bright;
Twining a riband in your hair,
Kissing good-bye you go down-stair
Then I'm as lonely as can be.
Oh, how I wish you were with me!
Yet when you go out on the street,
Mother, there's always lots to eat." . . .

II

For days the igloo has been dark;
But now the rag wick sends a spark
That glitters in the icy air,
And wakes frost sapphires everywhere;

Bright, bitter flames, that adder-like
Dart here and there, yet fear to strike
The gruesome gloom wherein *they* lie,
My comrades, oh, so keen to die!
And I, the last—well, here I wait
The clock to strike the hour of eight. . . .

> *"Boy, it is bitter to be hurled*
> *Nameless and naked on the world;*
> *Frozen by night and starved by day,*
> *Curses and kicks and clouts your pay.*
> *But you must fight! Boy, look on me!*
> *Anarch of all earth-misery;*
> *Beggar and tramp and shameless sot;*
> *Emblem of ill, in rags that rot.*
> *Would you be foul and base as I?*
> *Oh, it is better far to die!*
> *Swear to me now you'll fight and fight,*
> *Boy, or I'll kill you here to-night."* . . .

III

Curse this silence soft and black!
Sting, little light, the shadows back!
Dance, little flame with freakish glee!
Twinkle with brilliant mockery!
Glitter on ice-robed roof and floor!
Jewel the bear-skin of the door!
Gleam in my beard, illume my breath,
Blanch the clock face that times my death!
But do not pierce that murk so deep,
Where in their sleeping-bags they sleep!
But do not linger where they lie,
They who had all the luck to die! . . .

> *"There is nothing more to say;*
> *Let us part and go our way.*

Since it seems we can't agree,
I will go across the sea.
Proud of heart and strong am I;
Not for woman will I sigh;
Hold my head up gay and glad;
You can find another lad." ...

IV

Above the igloo piteous flies
Our frayed flag to the frozen skies.
Oh, would you know how earth can be
A hell—go north of Eighty-three!
Go, scan the snows day after day,
And hope for help, and pray and pray;
Have seal-hide and sea-lice to eat;
Melt water with your body's heat;
Sleep all the fell, black winter through
Beside the dear, dead men you knew.
(The walrus blubber flares and gleams—
O God! how long a minute seems!) ...

"Mary, many a day has passed,
  Since that morn of hot-head youth.
Come I back at last, at last,
  Crushed with knowing of the truth;
How through bitter, barren years
  You loved me, and me alone;
Waited, wearied, wept your tears—
  Oh, could I atone, atone,
I would pay a million-fold!
  Pay you for the love you gave.
Mary, look down as of old—
  I am kneeling by your grave." ...

V

Olaf, the Blonde, was the first to go;
Bitten his eyes were by the snow;
Sightless and sealed his eyes of blue,
So that he died before I knew.
Here in these poor weak arms he died:
"Wolves will not get you, lad," I lied;
"For I will watch till Spring come round;
Slumber you shall beneath the ground."
Oh, how I lied! I scarce can wait:
Strike, little clock, the hour of eight! . . .

> *"Comrade, can you blame me quite?*
> *The horror of the long, long night*
> *Is on me, and I've borne with pain*
> *So long, and hoped for help in vain.*
> *So frail am I, and blind and dazed;*
> *With scurvy sick, with silence crazed.*
> *Beneath the Arctic's heel of hate,*
> *Avid for Death I wait, I wait.*
> *Oh, if I falter, fail to fight,*
> *Can you, dear comrade, blame me quite?"*

VI

Big Eric gave up months ago.
But seldom do men suffer so.
His feet sloughed off, his fingers died,
His hands shrank up and mummified.
I had to feed him like a child;
Yet he was valiant, joked and smiled,
Talked of his wife and little one
(Thanks be to God that I have none),
Passed in the night without a moan,
Passed, and I'm here alone, alone. . . .

"I've got to kill you, Dick.
Your life for mine, you know.
Better to do it quick.
A swift and sudden blow.
See! here's my hand to lick;
A hug before you go—
God! but it makes me sick;
Old dog, I love you so.
Forgive, forgive me, Dick—
A swift and sudden blow."

VII

Often I start up in the dark,
   Thinking the sound of bells to hear.
Often I wake from sleep: "Oh, hark!
   Help . . . it is coming . . . near and near."
Blindly I reel toward the door;
   There the snow billows bleak and bare;
Blindly I seek my den once more,
   Silence and darkness and despair.
Oh, it is all a dreadful dream!
   Scurvy and cold and death and dearth;
I will awake to warmth and gleam,
   Silvery seas and greening earth.
Life is a dream, its wakening,
Death, gentle shadow of God's wing. . . .

"Tick, little clock, my life away!
Even a second seems a day.
Even a minute seems a year,
Peopled with ghosts that press and peer
Into my face so charnel white,
Lit by the devilish, dancing light.
Tick, little clock! mete out my fate:
Tortured and tense I wait, I wait." . . .

VIII

Oh, I have sworn! the hour is nigh:
When it strikes eight I die, I die.
Raise up the gun—it stings my brow—
When it strikes eight . . . all ready . . . *now*—

.   .   .   .

Down from my hand the weapon dropped;
Wildly I stared . . .
      THE CLOCK HAD STOPPED.

IX

Phantoms and fears and ghosts have gone.
  Peace seems to nestle in my brain.
Lo! the clock stopped, I'm living on;
  Heart-sick I was, and less than sane.

Yet do I scorn the thing I planned,
  Hearing a voice: "O coward, fight!"
Then the clock stopped . . . whose was the hand?
  Maybe 'twas God's—ah, well, all's right.
Heap on me darkness, fold on fold!
  Pain! wrench and rack me! What can I?
Leap on me, hunger, thirst and cold!
  I will await my time to die;
Looking to Heaven that shines above;
Looking to God, and love . . . and love.

X

Hark! what is that? Bells, dogs again!
  Is it a dream? I sob and cry.
See! the door opens, fur-clad men
  Rush to my rescue; frail am I;

Feeble and dying, dazed and glad.
　　There is the pistol where it dropped.
"Boys, it was hard—but I'm not mad . . .
　　Look at the clock—it stopped, it stopped.
Carry me out. The heaven's smile.
　　See there's an arch of gold above.
Now, let me rest a little while—
　　Looking to God and love . . . and love."

*　　*　　*

While the Bannock Bakes

LIGHT up your pipe again, old chum, and sit awhile
　　with me;
　　I've got to watch the bannock bake—how restful is the air!
You'd little think that we were somewhere north of Sixty-
　　three.
　　Though where I don't exactly know, and don't precisely
　　care.
The man-size mountains palisade us round on every side;
　　The river is a-flop with fish, and ripples silver-clear;
The midnight sunshine brims yon cleft—we think it's the
　　Divide;
　　We'll get there in a month, maybe, or maybe in a year.

It doesn't matter, does it, pal? We're of that breed of men
　　With whom the world of wine and cards and women
　　disagree;
Your trouble was a roofless game of poker now and then,
　　And "raising up my elbow," that's what got away with
　　me.
We're merely "Undesirables," artistic more or less;

My horny hands are Chopin-wise; you quote your Brown-
ing well;
And yet we're fooling round for gold in this damned wilder-
ness :
The joke is, if we found it, we would both go straight to
hell.
Well, maybe we won't find it—and at least we've got the
"life."
We're both as brown as berries, and could wrestle with a
bear:
(That bannock's rising nicely, pal; just jab it with your
knife.)
Fine specimens of manhood they would reckon us out
there.
It's the tracking and the packing and the poling in the sun;
It's the sleeping in the open, it's the rugged, unfaked, food;
It's the snow-shoe and the paddle, and the camp-fire and the
gun,
And when I think of what I was, I know that it is good.

Just think of how we've poled all day up this strange little
stream;
Since life began no eye of man has seen this place before;
How fearless all the wild things are! the banks with goose-
grass gleam,
And there's a bronzy muskrat sitting sniffing at his door.
A mother duck with brook of ten comes squattering along;
The tawny, white-winged ptarmigan are flying all about;
And in that swirly, golden pool, a restless, gleaming throng,
The trout are waiting till we condescend to take them out.

Ah, yes, it's good! I'll bet that there's no doctor like the Wild:
(Just turn that bannock over there; it's getting nicely
brown):
I might be in my grave by now, forgotten and reviled,
Or rotting like a sickly cur in some far, foreign town.

I might be that vile thing I was—it all seems like a dream;
  I owed a man a grudge one time that only life could pay;
And yet it's half-forgotten now—how petty these things
    seem!
  (But that's "another story," pal; I'll tell it you some day.)

How strange two "irresponsibles" should chum away up
    here;
  But round the Arctic Circle friends are few and far
    between.
We've shared the same camp-fire and tent for nigh on seven
    year,
  And never had a word that wasn't cheering and serene.
We've halved the toil and split the spoil, and borne each
    other's pack;
  By all the Wild's freemasonry we're brothers, tried and
    true;
We've swept on danger side by side, and fought it back to
    back,
  And you would die for me, old pal, and I would die for you.

Now there was that time I got lost in Rory Bory Land,
  (How quick the blizzards sweep on one across that Polar
    sea!)
You formed a rescue crew of One, and saw a frozen hand
  That stuck out of a drift of snow—and, partner, it was Me.
But I got even, did I not, that day the paddle broke?
  White water on the Coppermine—a rock—a split canoe—
Two fellows struggling in the foam (one couldn't swim a
    stroke):
  A half-drowned man I dragged ashore . . . and, partner, it
    was You.

    .   .   .   .   .

In Rory Borealis Land the winter's long and black;
  The silence seems a solid thing, shot through with wolfish
    woe;

And rowelled by the eager stars the skies vault vastly back,
  And man seems but a little mite in that weird-lit plateau.
Nothing to do but smoke and yarn of wild and misspent lives,
  Beside the camp-fire there we sat—what tales you told to
    me
Of love and hate, and chance and fate, and temporary wives!
  In Rory Borealis Land, beside the Arctic Sea.

One yarn you told me in those days I can remember still;
  It seemed as if I visioned it, so sharp you sketched it in;
Bellona was the name, I think; a coast town in Brazil,
  Where nobody did anything but serenade and sin.
I saw it all—the jewelled sea, the golden scythe of sand,
  The stately pillars of the palms, the feathery bamboo,
The red-roofed houses and the swart, sun-dominated land,
  The people ever children, and the heavens ever blue.

You told me of that girl of yours, that blossom of old Spain,
  All glamour, grace and witchery, all passion, verve and
    glow.
How maddening she must have been! You made me see her
    plain,
  There by our little camp-fire, in the silence and the snow.
You loved her and she loved you. She'd a husband too, I
    think;
  A doctor chap, you told me, whom she treated like a dog,
A white man living on the beach, a hopeless slave to drink—
  (Just turn that bannock over there, that's propped against
    the log.)

That story seemed to strike me, pal—it happens every day:
  You had to go away awhile, then somehow it befell
The doctor chap discovered, gave her up, and went away;
  You came back, tired of her in time . . . there's nothing more
    to tell.

Hist! see those willows silvering where swamp and river
   meet!
  Just reach me up my rifle, quick; that's Mister Moose, I
    know—
There now, *I've got him dead to rights* ... but, hell! we've lots
   to eat!
  I don't believe in taking life—we'll let the beggar go.

Heigh-ho! I'm tired; the bannock's cooked; it's time we both
   turned in.
  The morning mist is coral-kissed, the morning sky is
    gold.
The camp-fire's a confessional — what funny yarns we
   spin!
  It sort of made me think a bit, that story that you told.
The fig-leaf belt and Rory Bory are such odd extremes,
  Yet after all how very small this old world seems to be ...
Yes, that was quite a yarn, old pal, and yet to me it seems
  You missed the point: the point is that the "doctor chap"
    ... was *me*.

*   *   *

Little Moccasins

COME out, O Little Moccasins, and frolic on the snow!
  Come out, O tiny beaded feet, and twinkle in the light!
I'll play the old Red River reel, you used to love it so:
  Awake, O Little Moccasins, and dance for me to-night!

Your hair was all a gleamy gold, your eyes a cornflower blue;
  Your cheeks were pink as tinted shells, you stepped light as
    a fawn,

Your mouth was like a coral bud, with seed pearls peeping
    through;
  As gladdening as Spring you were, as radiant as dawn.

Come out, O Little Moccasins! I'll play so soft and low,
  The songs you loved, the old heart-songs that in my
    mem'ry ring;
O child, I want to hear you now beside the camp-fire glow!
  With all your heart a-throbbing in the simple words you
    sing.

For there was only you and I, and you were all to me;
  And round us were the barren lands, but little did we fear;
Of all God's happy, happy folks the happiest were we . . .
  (Oh, call her, poor old fiddle mine, and maybe she will
    hear!)

Your mother was a half-breed Cree, but you were white all
    through;
  And I your father was—but, well, that's neither here nor
    there;
I only know, my little Queen, that all my world was you,
  And now that world can end to-night, and I will never care.

For there's a tiny wooden cross that pricks up through the
    snow:
  (Poor little Moccasins! you're tired, and so you lie at rest.)
And there's a grey-haired, weary man beside the camp-fire
    glow:
  (O fiddle mine! the tears to-night are drumming on your
    breast.)

The Squaw-man

THE cow-moose comes to water, and the beaver's overbold,
   The net is in the eddy of the stream;
The tepee stars the vivid sward with russet, red and gold,
   And in the velvet gloom the fire's agleam.
The night is ripe with quiet, rich with incense of the pine;
   From sanctuary lake I hear the loon:
The peaks are bright against the blue, and drenched with
     sunset wine,
   And like a silver bubble is the moon.

Cloud-high I climbed but yesterday; a hundred miles around
   I looked to see a rival fire agleam.
As in a crystal lens it lay, a land without a bound.
   All lure, and virgin vastitude, and dream.
The great sky roared exultantly, the great earth bared its
     breast,
   All river-veined and patterned with the pine;
The heedless hordes of caribou were streaming to the West,
   A land of lustrous mystery—and mine.

Yea, mine to frame my Odyssey: Oh, little do they know
   My conquest and the kingdom that I keep!
The meadows of the musk-ox where the laughing grasses
     grow,
   The rivers where the careless conies leap.
Beyond the silent Circle, where white men are fierce and few,
   I lord it, and I mock at man-made law;
Like a flame upon the water is my little light canoe,
   And yonder in the fireglow is my squaw.

A squaw-man! yes, that's what I am; sneer at me if you will.
    I've gone the grilling pace that cannot last;
With bawdry, bridge and brandy—Oh, I've drunk enough
      to kill
    A dozen such as you, but that is past.
I've swung round to my senses, found the place where I
      belong;
    The City made a madman out of me;
But beyond the Circle, where there's neither right nor wrong,
    I leap from life's strait-jacket, and I'm free.

Yet ever in the far forlorn, by trails of lone desire;
    Yet ever in the dawn's white leer of hate;
Yet ever by the dripping kill, beside the drowsy fire,
    There comes the fierce heart-hunger for a mate.
There comes the mad blood-clamour for a woman's clinging
      hand,
    Love-humid eyes, the velvet of a breast:
And so I sought the Bonnet-plumes, and chose from out the
      band
    The girl I thought the sweetest and the best.

O wistful women I have loved before my dark disgrace!
    O women fair and rare in my home land!
Dear ladies, if I saw you now I'd turn away my face,
    Then crawl to kiss your footprints in the sand!
And yet—that day the rifle jammed—a wounded moose at
      bay—
    A roar, a charge . . . I faced it with my knife:
A shot from out the willow-scrub, and there the monster
      lay...
    Yes, little Laughing Eyes, you saved my life.

The man must have the woman, and we're all brutes more
      or less,
    Since first the male ape shinned the family tree;

And yet I think I love her with a husband's tenderness,
    And yet I know that she would die for me.
Oh, if I left you, Laughing Eyes, and nevermore came back,
    God help you, girl! I know what you would do . . .
I see the lake wan in the moon, and from the shadow black,
    There drifts a little *empty* birch canoe.

We're here beyond the Circle, where there's never wrong
        nor right;
    We aren't spliced according to the law;
But by the gods I hail you on this hushed and holy night
    As the mother of my children, and my squaw.
I see your little slender face set in the firelight glow;
    I pray that I may never make it sad;
I hear you croon a baby song, all slumber-soft and low—
    God bless you, little Laughing Eyes! I'm glad.

*   *   *

I'm Scared of it All

I'M scared of it all, God's truth! so I am:
    It's too big and brutal for me.
My nerve's on the raw and I don't give a damn
    For all the "hoorah" that I see.
I'm pinned between subway and overhead train,
    Where automobillies swoop down;
Oh, I want to go back to the timber again—
    I'm scared of the terrible town.

I want to go back to my lean, ashen plains;
    My rivers that flash into foam;

My ultimate valleys where solitude reigns;
   My trail from Fort Churchill to Nome.
My forests packed full of mysterious gloom,
   My ice-fields agrind and aglare:
The city is deadfalled with danger and doom—
   I know that I'm safer up there.

I watch the wan faces that flash in the street:
   All kinds and all classes I see.
Yet never a one in the million I meet
   Has the smile of a comrade for me.
Just jaded and panting like dogs in a pack;
   Just tensed and intent on the goal:
O God! but I'm lonesome—I wish I was back,
   Up there in the land of the Pole.

I wish I was back on the Hunger Plateaus,
   And seeking the lost caribou;
I wish I was up where the Coppermine flows
   To the kick of my little canoe,
I'd like to be far on some weariful shore,
   In the land of the Blizzard and Bear:
Oh, I wish I was snug in the Arctic once more,
   For I know I am safer up there!

I prowl in the canyons of dismal unrest;
   I cringe—I'm so weak and so small.
I can't get my bearings, I'm crushed and oppressed
   With the haste and the waste of it all.
The slaves and the madmen, the lust and the sweat,
   The fear in the faces I see;
The getting, the spending, the fever, the fret—
   It's too bleeding cruel for me.

I feel it's all wrong, but I can't tell you why—
   The palace, the hovel next door;

The insolent towers that sprawl to the sky,
    The crush and the rush and the roar.
I'm trapped like a fox and I fear for my pelt;
    I cower in the crash and the glare;
Oh, I want to be back in the avalanche belt,
    For I know that it's safer up there!

I'm scared of it all. Oh, afar I can hear
    The voice of my solitudes call!
We're nothing but brute with a little veneer,
    And nature is best after all.
There's tumult and terror abroad in the street;
    There's menace and doom in the air;
I've got to get back to my thousand-mile beat;
    The trail where the cougar and silver-tip meet;
The snows and the camp-fire, with wolves at my feet;
    Good-bye, for it's safer up there.

To be forming good habits up there;
To be starving on rabbits up there;
    In your hunger and woe,
    Though it's sixty below,
Oh, I know that it's safer up there!

*   *   *

The Song of the Camp-fire

I

HEED me, feed me, I am hungry, I am red-tongued with
    desire;
    Boughs of balsam, slabs of cedar, gummy faggots of the
    pine,

Heap them on me, let me hug them, to my eager heart of fire,
  Roaring, soaring up to heaven as a symbol and a sign.
Bring me knots of sunny maple, silver birch and tamarack;
  Leaping, sweeping, I will lap them with my ardent wings
    of flame;
I will kindle them to glory, I will beat the darkness back;
  Streaming, gleaming, I will goad them to my glory and my
    fame.
Bring me gnarly limbs of live-oak, aid me in my frenzied
    fight;
  Strips of iron-wood, scaly blue-gum, writhing redly in
    my hold;
With my lunge of lurid lances, with my whips that flail the
    night,
  They will burgeon into beauty, they will foliate in gold.
Let me star the dim sierras, stab with light the inland seas;
  Roaming wind and roaring darkness! seek no mercy at my
    hands;
I will mock the marly heavens, lamp the purple prairies,
  I will flaunt my deathless banners down the far, unhouseled
    lands.
In the vast and vaulted pine-gloom where the pillared forests
    frown,
  By the sullen, brutish rivers running where God only
    knows,
On the starlit coral beaches when the combers thunder
    down,
  In the death-spell of the barrens, in the shudder of the
    snows;
In a blazing belt of triumph from the palm-leaf to the pine,
  As a symbol of defiance, lo! the wilderness I span;
And my beacons burnt exultant as an everlasting sign
  Of unending domination, of the mastery of Man;
I, the Life, the fierce Uplifter, I that weaned him from the
    mire;
  I, the angel and the devil; I, the tyrant and the slave;

I, the Spirit of the Struggle; I, the mighty God of Fire;
   I, the Maker and Destroyer; I, the Giver and the Grave.

II

Gather round me, boy and grey-beard, frontiersmen of every
   kind.
Few are you, and far and lonely, yet an army forms behind:
By your camp-fires shall they know you, ashes scattered
   to the wind.

Peer into my heart of solace, break your bannock at my
   blaze;
Smoking, stretched in lazy shelter, build your castles as
   you gaze;
Or, it may be, deep in dreaming, think of dim, unhappy days.

Let my warmth and glow caress you, for your trails are grim
   and hard;
Let my arms of comfort press you hunger-hewn and battle-
   scarred:
O my lovers! how I bless you with your lives so madly
   marred!

For you seek the silent spaces, and their secret lore you
   glean;
For you win the savage races, and the brutish Wild you
   wean;
And I gladden desert places, where camp-fire has never
   been.

From the Pole unto the Tropics is there trail ye have not
   dared?
And because you hold death lightly, so by death shall you be
   spared,
(As the sages of the ages in their pages have declared.)

On the roaring Arkilinik in a leaky bark canoe;
Up the cloud of Mount McKinley, where the avalanche
 leaps through;
In the furnace of Death Valley, when the mirage glimmers
 blue.

Now a smudge of wiry willows on the weary Kuskoquim;
Now a flare of gummy pine-knots where Vancouver's scaur is
 grim;
Now a gleam of sunny ceiba, when the Cuban beaches dim.

Always, always God's Great Open: lo! I burn with keener
 light
In the corridors of silence, in the vestibules of night;
'Mid the ferns and grasses gleaming, was there ever gem so
 bright?

Not for weaklings, not for women, like my brother of the
 hearth;
Ring your songs of wrath around me, I was made for manful
 mirth,
In the lusty, gusty greatness, on the bald spots of the earth.

Men, my masters! Men, my lovers! ye have fought and ye
 have bled;
Gather round my ruddy embers, softly glowing is my
 bed;
By my heart of solace dreaming, rest ye and be comforted!

III

I am dying, O my masters! by my fitful flame ye sleep;
 My purple plumes of glory droop forlorn.
Grey ashes choke and cloak me, and above the pines there
 creep
 The stealthy silver moccasins of morn.

There comes a countless army, it's the Legion of the Light;
  It tramps in gleaming triumph round the world;
And before its jewelled lances all the shadows of the night
  Back in to abysmal darknesses are hurled.

Leap to life again, my lovers! ye must toil and never tire;
  The day of daring, doing, brightens clear,
When the bed of spicy cedar and the jovial camp-fire
  Must only be a memory of cheer.
There is hope and golden promise in the vast portentous
    dawn;
  There is glamour in the glad, effluent sky:
Go and leave me; I will dream of you and love you when
    you're gone;
  I have served you, O my masters! let me die.

A little heap of ashes, grey and sodden by the rain,
  Wind-scattered, blurred and blotted by the snow :
Let that be all to tell of me, and glorious again,
  Ye things of greening gladness, leap and glow!
A black scar in the sunshine by the palm-leaf or the pine,
  Blind to the night and dead to all desire;
Yet oh, of life and uplift what a symbol and a sign!
  Yet oh, of power and conquest what a destiny is mine!
A little heap of ashes—Yea! a miracle divine,
  The footprint of a god, all-radiant Fire.

The Ballad of Salvation Bill

'TWAS in the bleary middle of the hard-boiled Arctic night,
I was lonesome as a loon, so if you can,
Imagine my emotions of amazement and delight
When I bumped into that Missionary Man.
He was lying lost and dying in the moon's unholy leer,
And frozen from his toes to finger-tips;
The famished wolf-pack ringed him; but he didn't seem to
    fear,
As he pressed his ice-bound Bible to his lips.

'Twas the limit of my trap-line, with the cabin miles away,
And every step was like a stab of pain;
But I packed him like a baby, and I nursed him night and
    day,
Till I got him back to health and strength again.

So there we were, benighted in the shadow of the Pole,
And he might have proved a priceless little pard,
If he hadn't got to worrying about my blessed soul,
And a-quotin' me his Bible by the yard.

Now there was I, a husky guy, whose god was Nicotine,
With a "coffin-nail" a fixture in my mug;
I rolled them in the pages of a pulpwood magazine,
And hacked them with my jack-knife from the plug.
For, Oh to know the bliss and glow that good tobacco means,
Just live among the everlasting ice. . . .
So judge my horror when I found my stock of magazines
Was chewed into a chowder by the mice.

A woeful week went by and not a single pill I had,
Me that would smoke my forty in a day;
I sighed, I swore, I strode the floor; I felt I would go
    mad:
The gospel-plugger watched me in dismay.
My brow was wet, my teeth were set, my nerves were rasping
    raw;
And yet that preacher couldn't understand:
So with despair I wrestled there—when suddenly I saw
The volume he was holding in his hand.

Then something snapped inside my brain, and with an evil
    start
The wolf-man in me woke to rabid rage.
"I saved your lousy life," says I; "so show you have a heart,
And tear me out a solitary page."
He shrank and shrivelled at my words; his face went pewter
    white;
'Twas just as if I'd handed him a blow;
And then . . . and then he seemed to swell, and grow to
    Heaven's height,
And in a voice that rang he answered: "No!"

I grabbed my loaded rifle and I jabbed it to his chest:
"Come on, you shrimp, give up that Book," says I.
Well sir, he was a parson, but he stacked up with the best,
And for grit I got to hand it to the guy.
"If I should let you desecrate this Holy Word," he said,
"My soul would be eternally accurst;
So go on, Bill, I'm ready. You can pump me full of lead
And take it, but—you've got to kill me first."

Now I'm no foul assassin, though I'm full of sinful ways,
And I knew right there the fellow had me beat;
For I felt a yellow mongrel in the glory of his gaze,
And I flung my foolish firearm at his feet.

Then wearily I turned away, and dropped upon my bunk,
And there I lay and blubbered like a kid.
"Forgive me, pard," says I at last, "for acting like a skunk,
But hide the blasted rifle. . . ." Which he did.

And he also hid his Bible, which was maybe just as well,
For the sight of all that paper gave me pain;
And there were crimson moments when I felt I'd go to hell
To have a single cigarette again.
And so I lay day after day, and brooded dark and deep,
Until one night I thought I'd end it all;
Then rough I roused the preacher, where he stretched pretending sleep,
With his map of horror turned towards the wall.

"See here, my pious pal," says I, "I've stood it long enough. . . .
Behold! I've mixed some strychnine in a cup;
Enough to kill a dozen men—believe me it's no bluff;
Now watch me, for I'm gonna drink it up.
You've seen me bludgeoned by despair through bitter days
and nights,
And now you'll see me squirming as I die.
You're not to blame, you've played the game according to
your lights. . . .
But how would Christ have played it?—Well, good-bye. . . ."

With that I raised the deadly drink and laid it to my lips,
But he was on me with a tiger-bound;
And as we locked and reeled and rocked with wild and wicked
grips,
The poison cup went crashing to the ground.
"Don't do it, Bill," he madly shrieked. "Maybe I acted
wrong.
See, here's my Bible—use it as you will;
But promise me—you'll read a little as you go along. . . .
You do! Then take it, Brother; smoke your fill."

And so I did. I smoked and smoked from Genesis to Job,
And as I smoked I read each blessed word;
While in the shadow of his bunk I heard him sigh and sob,
And then . . . a most peculiar thing occurred.
I got to reading more and more, and smoking less and less,
Till just about the day his heart was broke,
Says I : "Here, take it back, me lad. I've had enough, I guess.
Your paper makes a mighty rotten smoke."

So then and there with plea and prayer he wrestled for my soul,
And I was racked and ravaged by regrets.
But God was good, for lo! next day there came the police
    patrol,
With paper for a thousand cigarettes. . . .
So now I'm called Salvation Bill; I teach the Living Law,
And bally-hoo the Bible with the best;
And if a guy won't listen—why, I sock him on the jaw
And preach the Gospel sitting on his chest.

•   •   •

The Ballad of Hank the Finn

NOW Fireman Flynn met Hank the Finn where lights of
    Lust-land glow;
"Let's leave," says he, "the lousy sea, and give the land a
    show.
I'm fed up to the molar mark with wallopin' the brine;
I feel the bloody barnacles a-carkin' on me spine.
Let's hit the hard-boiled North a crack, where creeks are
    paved with gold."
' You count me in," says Hank the Finn. "Ay do as Ay ban
    told."

And so they sought the Lonely Land and drifted down its
    stream,
Where sunny silence round them spanned, as dopey as a
    dream.
But to the spell of flood and fell their gold-rimmed eyes were
    blind;
By pine and peak they paused to seek, but nothing did they
    find;
No yellow glint of dust to mint, just mud and mocking
    sand,
And a hateful hush that seemed to crush them down on
    every hand.
Till Fireman Flynn grew mean as sin, and cursed his
    comrade cold,
But Hank the Finn would only grin, and. . . do as he was
    told.

Now Fireman Flynn had pieces ten of yellow Yankee gold,
Which every night he would invite his partner to behold.
"Look hard," says he; "It's all you'll see in this god-blasted
    land;
But don't you fret, I'm gonna let you hold them in your hand.
Yeah! Watch 'em gleam then go and *dream* they're yours to
    have and hold."
Then Hank the Finn would scratch his chin and . . . do as he
    was told.

But every night by camp-fire light, he'd incubate his woes,
And fan the hate of mate for mate, the evil Arctic knows.
In dreams the Lapland witches gloomed like gargoyles
    overhead,
While the devils three of Helsinskee came cowering by his
    bed.
"Go, take," said they, "the yellow loot he's clinking in his
    belt,
And leave the sneaking wolverines to snout around his pelt.

Last night he called you *Swedish* scum, from out the glory-
   hole;
To-day he said you were a bum, and damned your mother's
   soul.
Go, plug with lead his scurvy head, and grab his greasy
   gold. . . ."
Then Hank the Finn saw red within, and . . . did as he was
   told.

So in due course the famous Force of Men Who Get Their
   Man,
Swooped down on sleeping Hank the Finn, and popped him
   in the can.
And in due time his grievous crime was judged without a plea,
And he was dated up to swing upon the gallows tree.
Then Sheriff gave a party in the Law's almighty name,
He gave a neck-tie party, and he asked me to the same.
There was no hooch a-flowin' and his party wasn't gay,
For O our hearts were heavy at the dawning of the day.
There was no band a-playin' and the only dancin' there
Was Hank the Finn interpretin' his solo on the air.

We climbed the scaffold steps and stood beside the knotted
   rope.
We watched the hooded hangman and his eyes were dazed
   with dope.
The Sheriff was in evening dress; a bell began to toll,
A beastly bell that struck a knell of horror to the soul.
As if the doomed one was myself, I shuddered, waiting
   there.
I spoke no word, then . . . then I heard *his* step upon the stair;
His halting foot, moccasin clad . . . and then I saw him stand
Between a weeping warder and a priest with Cross in hand.
And at the sight a murmur rose of terror and of awe,
And all them hardened gallows fans were sick at what they
   saw:

For as he towered above the mob, his limbs with leather
    triced,
By all that's wonderful, I swear, *his face was that of Christ.*

Now I ain't no blaspheming cuss, so don't you start to shout.
You see, his beard had grown so long it framed his face about.
His rippling hair was long and fair, his cheeks were spirit-
    pale,
His face was bright with holy light that made us wince and
    quail.
He looked at us with eyes a-shine, and sore were we confused,
As if he were the Judge divine, and we were the accused.
Aye, as serene he stood between the hangman and the cord,
You would have sworn, with anguish torn, he was the Blessed
    Lord.

The priest was wet with icy sweat, the Sheriff's lips were dry,
And we were staring starkly at the man who had to die.
"Lo! I am raised above you all," his pale lips seemed to say,
"For in a moment I shall leap to God's Eternal Day.
Am I not happy! I forgive you each for what you do;
Redeemed and penitent I go, with heart of love for you."

So there he stood in mystic mood, with scorn sublime of
    death.
I saw him gently kiss the Cross, and then I held my breath.
That blessed smile was blotted out; they dropped the hood
    of black;
They fixed the noose around his neck, the rope was hanging
    slack.
I heard him pray, I saw him sway then . . . then he was not
    there;
A rope, a ghastly yellow rope was jerking in the air;
A jigging rope that soon was still; a hush as of the tomb,
And Hank the Finn, that man of sin, had met his rightful
    doom.

His rightful doom! Now that's the point. I'm wondering,
    because
I hold *a man is what he is,* and never what he was.
You see, the priest had filled that guy so full of holy dope,
That at the last he came to die as pious as the Pope.
A gentle ray of sunshine made a halo round his head.
I thought to see a sinner—lo! I saw a Saint instead.
Aye, as he stood as martyrs stand, clean-cleansed of mortal
    dross,
I think he might have gloried had ... WE NAILED HIM TO A
    CROSS.

*   *   *

Touch-the-Button Nell

Beyond the Rocking Bridge it lies, the burg of evil fame,
The huts where hive and swarm and thrive the sisterhood of
    shame.
Through all the night each cabin light goes out and then goes in,
A blood-red heliograph of lust, a semaphore of sin.
From Dawson Town, soft skulking down, each lewdster seeks his
    mate;
And glad and bad, kimono clad, the wanton women wait.
The Klondike gossips to the moon, and simmers o'er its bars;
Each silent hill is dark and chill, and chill the patient stars.
Yet hark! upon the Rocking Bridge a baccanalian step;
A whispered: "Come," the skirt of some hell-raking demirep....

.   .   .   .   .

They gave a dance in Lousetown, and the Tenderloin was
    there,
The girls were fresh and frolicsome, and nearly all were fair.

They flaunted on their backs the spoil of half-a-dozen
  towns;
And some they blazed in gems of price, and some wore Paris
  gowns.
The voting was divided as to who might be the belle;
But all opined, the winsomest was Touch-the-Button Nell.

Among the merry mob of men was one who did not dance,
But watched the "light fantastic" with a sour and sullen
  glance.
They saw his white teeth grit and gleam, they saw his thick
  lips twitch;
They knew him for the giant Slav, one Riley Dooleyvitch.

"Oh Riley Dooleyvitch, come forth," quoth Touch-the-
  Button Nell,
"And dance a step or two with me—the music's simply
  swell."
He crushed her in his mighty arms, a meek, beguiling witch:
"With you, Oh Nell, I'd dance to Hell," said Riley Dooley-
  vitch.

He waltzed her up, he waltzed her down, he waltzed her
  round the hall;
His heart was putty in her hands, his very soul was thrall.
As Antony of old succumbed to Cleopatra's spell,
So Riley Dooleyvitch bowed down to Touch-the-Button
  Nell.

"And do you love me true?" she cried. "I love you as my life."
"How can you prove your love?" she sighed. "I beg you, be
  my wife.
I stake big pay up Hunker way; some day I be so rich;
I make you shine in satins fine," said Riley Dooleyvitch.

"Some day you'll be so rich," she mocked; "That old pipe-
    dream don't go.
Who gets an option on this kid must have the coin to show.
You work your ground. When Spring comes round, our
    wedding bells will ring.
I'm on the square, and *I'll* take care of all the gold you bring."

So Riley Dooleyvitch went back and worked upon his claim;
He ditched and drifted, sunk and stoped, with one unswerv-
    ing aim;
And when his poke of raw moose-hide with dust began to
    swell,
He brought and laid it at the feet of Touch-the-Button Nell.

.   .   .   .   .

Now like all others of her ilk, the lady had a friend,
And what she made by way of trade, she gave to him to spend;
To stake him in a poker game, or pay his barroom score:
He was a pimp from Paris, and his name was Lew Lamore.

And so as Dooleyvitch went forth and worked as he was bid,
And wrested from the frozen muck the yellow stuff it hid,
And brought it to his Lady Nell, she gave him love galore
But handed over all her gains to festive Lew Lamore.

.   .   .   .   .

A year had gone, a weary year of strain and bloody sweat;
Of pain and hurt in dark and dirt, of fear that she forget.
He sought once more her cabin door: "I've laboured like a
    beast;
But now, dear one, the time has come to go before the priest.

"I've brought you gold—a hundred-fold I'll bring you
    by-and-by;
But Oh I want you, want you bad; I want you till I die.

Come, quit this life with evil rife—we'll joy while yet we
    can. . . ."
"I may not wed with you," she said, "I love another man.

"I love him and I hate him so. He holds me in a spell.
He beats me—see my bruised breast; he makes my life a hell.
He bleeds me, as by sin and shame I earn my daily bread:
Oh cruel Fate, I cannot mate till Lew Lamore be dead!"

    .   .   .   .   .

The long, lean flume streaked down the hill, five hundred feet
    of fall;
The waters in the dam above chafed at their prison wall;
They surged and swept, they churned and leapt, with savage
    glee and strife;
With spray and spume the dizzy flume thrilled like a thing of
    life.

"We must be free," the waters cried, and scurried down the
    slope;
"No power can hold us back," they roared, and hurried in
    their hope.
Into a mighty pipe they plunged; like maddened steers they
    ran,
And crashed out through a shard of steel—to serve the will of
    Man.

And there, hydraulicing his ground beside a bed-rock ditch,
With eye aflame and savage aim was Riley Dooleyvitch.
In long hip-boots and overalls, and dingy denim shirt,
Behind a giant monitor he pounded at the dirt.

A steely shaft of water shot, and smote the face of clay;
It burrowed in the frozen muck, and scooped the dirt away;
It gored the gravel from its bed, it bellowed like a bull;
It hurled the heavy rocks aloft like heaps of fleecy wool.

Strength of a hundred men was there, resistless might and
    skill,

And only Riley Dooleyvitch to swing it at his will.
He played it up, he played it down, nigh deafened by its roar,
'Till suddenly he raised his eyes, and there stood Lew
    Lamore.

Pig-eyed and heavy jowled he stood, and puffed a big cigar;
As cool as though he ruled the roost in some Montmartre bar.
He seemed to say: "I've got a cinch, a double diamond
    hitch:
I'll skin this Muscovitish oaf, this Riley Dooleyvitch."

He shouted: "Stop ze water gun; it stun me . . . *Sacré dam!*
I like to make one beezeness deal; you know ze man I am.
Zat leetle girl, she love me so—I tell you what I do:
You geeve to me zees claim. . . . *Jeezcrize!* I geeve zat girl
    to you."

"I'll see you damned," says Dooleyvitch; but e'er he checked
    his tongue,
(It *may* have been an accident) the "Little Giant" swung;
Swift as a lightning flash it swung, until it plumply bore
And met with an obstruction in the shape of Lew Lamore.

It caught him up, and spun him round, and tossed him like a
    ball;
It played and pawed him in the air, before it let him fall.
Then just to show what it could do, with savage rend and
    thud,
It ripped the entrails from his spine, and dropped him in the
    mud.

They gathered up the broken bones, and sadly in a sack,
They bore to town the last remains of Lew Lamore, the
    macque.
And would you hear the full details of how it all befell,
Ask Missis Riley Dooleyvitch (late Touch-the-Button Nell).

The Ice-Worm Cocktail

TO Dawson Town came Percy Brown from London on the
    Thames.
A pane of glass was in his eye, and stockings on his stems.
Upon the shoulder of his coat a leather pad he wore,
To rest his deadly rifle when it wasn't seeking gore;
The which it must have often been, for Major Percy Brown,
According to his story was a hunter of renown,
Who in the Murrumbidgee wilds had stalked the kangaroo
And killed the cassowary on the plains of Timbuctoo
And now the Arctic fox he meant to follow to its lair,
And it was also his intent to beard the Arctic hare....
Which facts concerning Major Brown I merely tell because
I fain would have you know him for the Nimrod that he was.

Now Skipper Grey and Deacon White were sitting in the
    shack,
And sampling of the whisky that pertained to Sheriff Black.
Said Skipper Grey: "I want to say a word about this Brown:
The piker's sticking out his chest as if he owned the town."
Said Sheriff Black: "He has no lack of frigorated cheek;
He called himself a Sourdough when he'd just been here a
    week."
Said Deacon White: "Methinks you're right, and so I have a
    plan
By which I hope to prove to-night the mettle of the man.
Just meet me where the hooch-bird sings, and though our
    ways be rude
We'll make a *proper* Sourdough of this Piccadilly dude."

Within the Malamute Saloon were gathered all the gang;
The fun was fast and furious, and loud the hooch-bird sang.
In fact the night's hilarity had almost reached its crown,
When into its storm-centre breezed the gallant Major Brown.
And at the apparition, with its glass eye and plus-fours.
From fifty alcoholic throats resounded fifty roars.
With shouts of stark amazement and with whoops of sheer
    delight,
They surged around the stranger, but the first was Deacon
    White.
"We welcome you," he cried aloud, "to this the Great White
    Land.
The Arctic Brotherhood is proud to grip you by the hand.
Yea, sportsman of the bull-dog breed, from trails of far away,
To Yukoners this is indeed a memorable day.
Our jubilation to express, vocabularies fail. . . .
Boys, hail the Great Cheechaco!" And the boys responded:
    "Hail!"

"And now," continued Deacon White to blushing Major
    Brown,
"Behold assembled the *eelight* and cream of Dawson Town.
And one ambition fills their hearts and makes their bosoms
    glow—
They want to make you, honoured sir, a *bony feed* Sourdough.
The same, some say, is one who's seen the Yukon ice go out,
But most profound authorities the definition doubt.
And to the genial notion of this meeting, Major Brown,
A Sourdough is a guy who drinks . . . an ice-worm cocktail
    down."

"By Gad!" responded Major Brown, "that's ripping, don't
    you know.
I've always felt I'd like to be a *certified* Sourdough.
And though I haven't any doubt your Winter's awf'ly nice,
Mayfair, I fear, may miss me ere the break-up of your ice.

Yet (pray excuse my ignorance of matters such as these)
A cocktail I can understand—but what's an ice-worm,
    please?"

Said Deacon White: "It is not strange that you should fail
    to know,
Since ice-worms are peculiar to the Mountain of Blue Snow.
Within the Polar rim it rears, a solitary peak,
And in the smoke of early Spring (a spectacle unique)
Like flame it leaps upon the sight and thrills you through and
    through,
For though its cone is piercing white, its base is blazing blue.
Yet all is clear as you draw near—for coyly peering out
Are hosts and hosts of tiny worms, each indigo of snout.

And as no nourishment they find, to keep themselves alive
They masticate each other's tails, till just the Tough survive.
Yet on this stern and Spartan fare so rapidly they grow,
That some attain six inches by the melting of the snow.
Then when the tundra glows to green and nigger-heads
    appear.
They burrow down and are not seen until another year.

"A toughish yarn," laughed Major Brown, "As well you may
    admit.
I'd like to see this little beast before I swallow it."
" 'Tis easy done," said Deacon White. "Ho! Barman, haste
    and bring
Us forth some pickled ice-worms of the vintage of last
    Spring."
But sadly still was Barman Bill, then sighed as one bereft:
"There's been a run on cocktails, Boss; there ain't an ice-
    worm left.
Yet wait. . . . By gosh! it seems to me that some of extra size
Were picked and put away to show the scientific guys."

Then deeply in a drawer he sought, and there he found a jar,
The which with due and proper pride he put upon the bar;
And in it, wreathed in queasy rings, or rolled into a ball,
A score of grey and greasy things were drowned in alcohol.
Their bellies were a bilious blue, their eyes a bulbous red;
Their backs were grey, and gross were they, and hideous of
head.
And when with gusto and a fork the barman speared one
out,
It must have gone four inches from its tail-tip to its snout.
Cried Deacon White with deep delight: "Say isn't that a
beaut?"
"I think it is," sniffed Major Brown, "a most disgustin' brute.
Its very sight gives me the pip. I'll bet my bally hat,
You're only spoofin' me, old chap, You'll never swallow
that."
"The hell I won't!" said Deacon White. "Hey! Bill, that
fellow's fine.
Fix up four ice-worm cocktails, and just put that wop in
mine."

So Barman Bill got busy, and with sacerdotal air
His art's supreme achievement he proceeded to prepare.
His silver cups, like sickle moon, went waving to and fro,
And four celestial cocktails soon were shining in a row.
And in the starry depths of each, artistically piled,
A fat and juicy ice-worm raised its mottled mug and smiled.
Then closer pressed the peering crowd, suspended was the
fun,
As Skipper Grey in courteous way said: "Stranger, please
take one."
But with a gesture of disgust the Major shook his head.
"You can't bluff me. You'll never drink that ghastly thing,"
he said.
"You'll see all right," said Deacon White, and held his cock-
tail high,

Till its ice-worm seemed to wiggle, and to wink a wicked eye.
Then Skipper Grey and Sheriff Black each lifted up a glass,
While through the tense and quiet crowd a tremor seemed to
   pass.
"Drink, Stranger, drink," boomed Deacon White. "Proclaim
   you're of the best,
A doughty Sourdough who has passed the Ice-Worm
   Cocktail Test."
And at these words, with all eyes fixed on gaping Major
   Brown,
Like a libation to the gods, each dashed his cocktail down.

The Major gasped with horror as the trio smacked their lips.
He twiddled at his eye-glass with unsteady finger-tips.
Into his starry cocktail with a look of woe he peered,
And its ice-worm, to his thinking, most incontinently leered.
Yet on him were a hundred eyes, though no one spoke
   aloud,
For hushed with expectation was the waiting, watching
   crowd.
The Major's fumbling hand went forth—the gang prepared
   to cheer;
The Major's falt'ring hand went back, the mob prepared to
   jeer.
The Major gripped his gleaming glass and laid it to his lips,
And as despairfully he took some nauseated sips,
From out its coil of crapulence the ice-worm raised its head;
Its muzzle was a murky blue, its eyes a ruby red.
And then a roughneck bellowed forth: "This stiff comes here
   and struts,
As if he'd bought the blasted North—jest let him show his
   guts."
And with a roar the mob proclaimed: "Cheechako, Major
   Brown,
Reveal that you're of Sourdough stuff, and drink your cock-
   tail down."

The Major took another look, then quickly closed his eyes,
For even as he raised his glass he felt his gorge arise.
Aye, even though his sight was sealed, in fancy he could see
That grey and greasy thing that reared and sneered in
mockery.
Yet round him ringed the callous crowd—and how they
seemed to gloat!
It must be done.... He swallowed hard.... The brute was
at his throat.
He choked... he gulped.... Thank God! at last he'd got the
horror down.
Then from the crowd went up a roar: "Hooray for Sour-
dough Brown!"
With shouts they raised him shoulder high, and gave a rous-
ing cheer,
But though they praised him to the sky the Major did not
hear.
Amid their demonstrative glee delight he seemed to lack;
Indeed it almost seemed that he—was "keeping something
back."
A clammy sweat was on his brow, and pallid as a sheet;
"I feel I must be going now," he'd plaintively repeat.
Aye, though with drinks and smokes galore, they tempted
him to stay,
With sudden bolt he gained the door, and made his get-a-way.

And ere next night his story was the talk of Dawson Town,
But gone and reft of glory was the wrathful Major Brown;
For that ice-worm (so they told him) of such formidable size
Was—*a stick of stained spaghetti with two red ink spots for eyes.*

The Leather Medal

ONLY a Leather Medal, hanging there on the wall,
Dingy and frayed and faded, dusty and worn and old;
Yet of my humble treasures I value it most of all,
And I wouldn't part with that medal if you gave me its weight
in gold.

Read the inscription: *For Valour—presented to Millie
MacGee.*
Ah! how in mem'ry it takes me back to the "auld lang syne,"
When Millie and I were sweethearts, and fair as a flower was
she—
Yet little I dreamt that her bosom held the heart of a heroine.

Listen! I'll tell you about it. . . . An orphan was Millie
MacGee,
Living with Billie her brother, under the Yukon sky.
Sam, her pa, was cremated in the winter of nineteen-three,
As duly and truly related by the pen of an author guy.

A cute little kid was Billie, solemn and silken of hair,
The image of Jackie Coogan in the days before movies could
speak.
Devoted to him was Millie, with more than a mother's care,
And happy were they together in their cabin on Bunker
Creek.

'Twas only a mining village, where hearts are simple and
true,

And Millie MacGee was schoolma'am, loved and admired by
    all;
Yet no one dreamed for a moment she'd do what she dared
    to do—
But wait and I'll try to tell you, as clear as I can recall. . . .

      .   .   .   .   .

Christmas Eve in the school-house! A scene of glitter and
    glee;
The children eager and joyful; parents and neighbours too;
Right in the forefront, Millie, close to the Christmas Tree,
While Billie, her brother, recited "The Shooting of Dan
    McGrew."

I reckon you've heard the opus, a ballad of guts and gore;
Of a Yukon frail and a frozen trail and a fight in a drinking
    dive.
It's on a par, I figger, with "The Face on the Bar Room
    Floor,"
And the boys who wrote them pieces ought to be skinned
    alive.

Picture that scene of gladness: the honest faces aglow;
The kiddies gaping and spellbound, as Billie strutted his stuff.
The stage with its starry candles, and there in the foremost
    row,
Millie, bright as a fairy, in radiant flounce and fluff.

More like an angel I thought her; all she needed was wings,
And I sought for a smile seraphic, but her eyes were only for
    Bill;
So there was I longing and loving, and dreaming the craziest
    things,
And Billie shouting and spouting, and everyone rapt and
    still.

Proud as a prince was Billie, bang in the footlights' glare,
And quaking for him was Millie, as she followed every word;

Then just as he reached the climax, ranting and sawing the
air—
Ugh! How it makes me shudder! The horrible thing
occurred. . . .

'Twas the day when frocks were frilly, and skirts were
scraping the ground,
And the snowy flounces of Millie like sea foam round her
swept;
Humbly adoring I watched her—when oh, my heart gave a
bound!
Hoary and scarred and hideous, out from the tree . . . IT . . .
crept.

A whiskered, beady-eyed monster, grisly and grim of hue;
Savage and slinking and silent, born of the dark and the dirt;
Dazed by the glare and the glitter, it wavered a moment or
two—
Then like a sinister shadow, it vanished . . . 'neath Millie's
skirt.

I stared. Had my eyes deceived me? I shivered. I held my
breath.
Surely I must have dreamed it? I quivered. I made to rise. . . .
Then—my God! it was real. Millie grew pale as death;
And oh, such a look of terror woke in her lovely eyes.

Did her scream ring out? Ah no, sir. It froze at her very lips.
Clenching her teeth she checked it, and I saw her slim hands
lock,
Grasping and gripping tensely, with desperate finger tips,
Something that writhed and wriggled under her dainty frock.

Quick I'd have dashed to her rescue, but fiercely she sig-
nalled: "No!"

Her eyes were dark with anguish, but her lips were set and
    grim;
Then I knew she was thinking of Billie—the kiddy must have
    his show,
Reap to the full his glory, nothing mattered but him.

So spiked to my chair with horror, there I shuddered and saw
Her fingers frenziedly clutching and squeezing with all their
    might
Something that squirmed and struggled, a demon of tooth
    and claw,
Fighting with fear and fury, under her garment white.

Oh could I only aid her! But the wide room lay between,
And again her eyes besought me: "Steady!" they seemed to
    say.
"Stay where you are, Bob Simmons; don't let us have a
    scene.
Billie will soon be finished. Only a moment . . . stay!"

A moment! Ah yes, I got her. I knew how night after night
She'd learned him each line of that ballad with patience and
    pride and glee;
With gesture and tone dramatic, she'd taught him how to
    recite. . . .
And now at the last to fail him—no, it must never be.

A moment! It seemed like ages. Why was Billie so slow?
He stammered. Twice he repeated: "The Lady that's
    known as Lou——"
The kiddy was stuck and she knew it. Her face was frantic
    with woe.
Could she but come to his rescue? Could she remember the
    cue?

I saw her whispering wildly as she leaned to the frightened
    boy;
But Billie stared like a dummy, and I stifled an anxious curse.
Louder, louder she prompted; then his face illumined with
    joy,
And panting, flushed and exultant, he finished the final verse.

So the youngster wound up like a whirlwind, while cheer
    resounded on cheer;
His piece was the hit of the evening. "Bravo!" I heard them
    say.
But there in the heart of the racket was one who could not
    hear—
The loving sister who'd coached him; for Millie had fainted
    away.

I rushed to her side and grabbed her; then others saw her
    distress,
And all were eager to aid me, as I pillowed that golden head.
But her arms were tense and rigid, and clutched in the folds
    of her dress,
Unlocking her hands they found it . . . A RAT *and the brute
    was dead.*

In silence she'd crushed its life out, rather than scare the
    crowd,
And queer little Billie's triumph. . . . Hey! Mother, what
    about tea?
I've just been telling a story that makes me so mighty
    proud. . . .
Stranger, let me present you—*my wife, that was Millie
    MacGee.*

A Sourdough Story

Hark to a Sourdough story, told at sixty below,
When the pipes are lit and we smoke and spit
Into the camp-fire glow.
Rugged are we and hoary, and statin' a general rule,
A genooine Sourdough story
Ain't no yarn for the Sunday School.

A Sourdough came to stake his claim in Heav'n one morning
    early.
Saint Peter cried: "Who waits outside them gates so bright
    and pearly?"
"I'm recent dead," the Sourdough said, "and crave to visit
    Hades,
Where haply pine some pals o' mine, includin' certain
    ladies."
Said Peter: "Go, you old Sourdough, from life so crooly
    riven;
And if we fail to find their trail, we'll have a snoop round
    Heaven."
He waved, and lo! that old Sourdough dropped down to
    Hell's red spaces;
But though 'twas hot he couldn't spot them old familiar faces.
The bedrock burned, and so he turned, and climbed with
    footsteps fleeter,
The stairway straight to Heaven's gate, and there, of course,
    was Peter.
"I cannot see my mates," sez he, "among those damned for-
    ever.

I have a hunch some of the bunch in Heaven I'll discover."

Said Peter: "True; and this I'll do (since Sourdoughs are
    my failing)

You see them guys in Paradise, lined up against the
    railing—

As bald as coots, in *birthday* suits, with beards below the
    middle. . . .

Well, I'll allow you in right now, if you can solve a riddle:

Among the gang of stiffs who hang and dodder round the
    portals,

Is one whose name is known to Fame—it's Adam, first of
    mortals.

For quiet's sake he makes a break from Eve, which is his
    Madame. . . .

Well, there's the gate.—To crash it straight, just spy the
    guy that's Adam."

The old Sourdough went down the row of greybeards
    ruminatin'.

With optics dim they peered at him, and pressed agin the
    gratin'.

In every face he sought some trace of our ancestral father;

But though he stared, he soon despaired the faintest clue to
    gather.

Then suddenly he whooped with glee: "Ha! Ha! an in-
    spiration."

And to and fro along the row he ran with animation.

To Peter, bold he cried: "Behold, all told there are eleven.

Suppose I fix on Number Six—say Boy! How's that for
    Heaven?"

"By Gosh! you win," said Pete, "Step in. But tell me how
    you chose him.

They're like as pins; all might be twins. There's nothing to
    disclose him."

The Sourdough said : " 'Twas hard; my head was seething
    with commotion.
I felt a dunce; then all at once I had a gorgeous notion.
I stooped and peered beneath each beard that drooped like
    fleece of mutton.
My search was crowned. . . . That bird I found—*ain't got no
    belly button.*"

*   *   *

Mc' Clusky's Nell

IN Mike Maloney's Nugget Bar the hooch was flowin' free,
An' One-eyed Mike was shakin' dice wi' Montreal Maree,
An' roarin' rageful warning when the boys got overwild,
When peekin' through the double door he spied a tiny child.
Then Mike Maloney muttered: "Hell! Now ain't that jest
    too bad;
It's Dud McClusky's orphan Nell a-lookin' for her dad,
An' him in back, a-lushin' wine wi' Violet de Vere—
Three times I've told the lousy swine to keep away from
    here."
"Pore leetle sing! He leave her lone, so he go on ze spree:
I feex her yet, zat Violet," said Montreal Maree.

Now I'm accommodatin' when it comes to scented sin
But when I saw that innocent step in our drunken din,
I felt that I would like to crawl an' hide my head in shame.
An' judgin' by their features all them sourdoughs felt the
    same.
For there they stood like chunks o' wood, forgettin' how to
    swear,
An' every glass o' likker was suspended in the air.

For with her hair of sunny silk, and big, blue pansy eyes
She looked jest like an angel child stepped outa paradise.
So then Big Mike, paternal like, took her upon his knee.
"Ze pauv' petite! She ees so sweet," said Montreal Maree.

The kid was mighty scared, we saw, an' peaked an' pale an'
    sad;
She nestled up to One-eyed Mike jest like he was her dad.
Then he got strokin' of her hair an' she began to sob,
An' there was anger in the air of all that plastered mob,
When in a hush so stark an' strained it seemed to stab the ear,
We heard the lush, punk-parlour laugh o' Violet de Vere.
Then Montreal Maree arose an' vanished from our sight,
An' soon we heard the sound o' blows suggestin' female fight.
An' when she joined the gang again dishevelly was she:
"Jeezecrize! I feex zat Violet," said Montreal Maree.

Then Barman Bill came forward with what seemed a glass o'
    milk:
"It's jest an egg-nog Missy, but it's slick an' smooth as silk."
An' as the kiddy slowly sipped wi' gaze o' glad surprise,
Them fifty sozzled sourdoughs uttered fifty happy sighs.
Then Ragtime Joe swung on his stool an' soft began to play
A liltin' tune that made ye think o' daffydills in May;
An' Gumboot Jones in solemn tones said: "You should hear
    her sing;
They've got the cabin next to mine, an' like a bird in Spring,
She fills that tumble-down old shack wi' simple melodee."
"Maybe she sing a song for us," said Montreal Maree.

Now I don't hold wi' mushy stuff, tear-jerkin' ain't my line,
Yet somehow that kid's singin' sent the shivers down my
    spine;
An' all them salted sourdoughs sighed, an' every eye was dim
For what she sang upon the bar was just a simple hymn;

Somethin' about "Abide with me, fast falls the eventide."
My Mother used to sing it—say, I listened bleary-eyed,
That childish treble was so sweet, so clear, so tender true,
It seemed to grip you by the heart an' did queer things to you.
It made me think o' childhood days from sin an' sorrow free:
"Zat child, she make me want to cry," said Montreal Maree.

Then up spoke One-eyed Mike: "We can't with us let her
    abide;
For her dear Mother's sake we gotta send that kid outside.
Ye know this camp's a den o' sin, ye know that Dud's no dice—
Let's stake her to a convent school, an' have her brought up
    nice."
An' so them bearded sourdoughs crowded round an' one an'
    all,
Dug down an' flung upon the bar their nuggets great an'
    small.
"I guess we got a thousand bucks," exulted One-eyed Mike;
"You bastards are a credit to the camp of Lucky Strike."
"You see zis leetle silver cross my mozzaire give to me—
Look boys, I hang it on zee *gosse*," said Montreal Maree.

Time marches on; that little Nell is now a famous star,
An' yet she got her singin' start on Mike Maloney's bar.
Aye, it was back in ninety-eight she made her first dayboo,
An' of that audience to-day are left but only two.
For all them bibulous sourdoughs have bravely passed away,
An' Lucky Strike is jest another ghost town of to-day.
But Nell now sings in opera, we saw her in Boheem;
'Twas at a high-toned matinay, an' say! she was a dream.
So also thought the white-haired dame a-sittin' down by me—
My lovin' spouse that once was known as Montreal Maree.

Ghosts

I TO a crumpled cabin came
Upon a hillside high,
And with me was a withered dame
As weariful as I.
"It used to be our home," said she;
"How I remember well!
Oh that our happy hearth should be
Today an empty shell!"

The door was flailing in the storm
That deafed us with its din;
The roof that kept us once so warm
Now let the snow-drift in.
The floor sagged to the sod below,
The walls caved crazily;
We only heard the wind of woe
Where once was glow and glee.

So there we stood disconsolate
Beneath the Midnight Dome,
An ancient miner and his mate,
Before our wedded home,
Where we had known such love and cheer . . .
I sighed, then soft she said :
"Do not regret—remember, dear,
We, too, are dead."

Dance Hall Girls

WHERE are the dames I used to know
In Dawson in the days of yore?
Alas, it's fifty years ago,
And most, I guess, have "gone before."
The swinging scythe is swift to mow
Alike the gallant and the fair;
And even I, with gouty toe,
Am glad to fill a rocking chair.

Ah me, I fear each gaysome girl
Who in champagne I used to toast,
Or cozen in the waltz's whirl,
Is now alas, a wistful ghost.
Oh where is Touch-The-button Nell?
Or Minnie Dale or Rosa Lee,
Or Lorna Doone or Daisy Bell?
And where is Montreal Maree?

Fair ladies of my lusty youth,
I fear that you are dead and gone:
Where's Gertie of the Diamond Tooth,
And where the Mare of Oregon?
What's come of Violet de Vere,
Claw-fingered Kate and Gumboot Sue?
They've crossed the Great Divide, I fear;
Remembered now by just a few.

A few who like myself can see
Through half a century of haze
A heap of goodness in their glee
And kindness in their wanton ways.
Alas, my sourdough days are dead,
Yet let me toss a tankard down ...
Here's hoping that you wed and bred,
And lives of circumspection led,
Gay dance-hall girls of Dawson Town!

* * *

Eldorado

I PITCHED my tent beneath a pine
Upon a grassy mound,
And all that summer worked my mine,
Yet never wealth I found;
Each night I dreamed of fortune dear,
Of pokes of virgin gold:
Alas! what riches were so near,
The grass roots could have told.

So broke and burdened with despair,
Abandoning my "lay,"
Believing that no gold was there,
I upped and went away;
And then a Swede came to my mound;
With careless pick he struck,
And where I slept a fortune found,
For that's the way of Luck.

God save us all from sudden wealth
That makes the head to swell;
Champagne and women mined his health
And he went plumb to hell.
And me? To win my bread I drive
A heavy highway truck. . . .
But he is dead and I'm alive,
—And that's the way of Luck.

*　　*　　*

Two Men
(J. L. and R. B.)

In the Northland there were three
Pukka pliers of the pen;
Two of them had Fame in fee
And were loud and lusty men;
By them like a shrimp was I—
Yet alas! they had to die.

Jack was genius through and through.
Who his future could foretell?
What we sweated blood to do
He would deem a bagatelle.
Yet in youth he had to die,
And an ancient man am I.

Rex was rugged as an oak;
Story-teller born was he.
First of writing, fighting folk,
How he lived prodigiously!
Better man he was than I,
Yet forlorn he had to die.

Jack was made of god-like stuff,
Born to battle for the right;
Rex of fighting had enough
When the gods destroyed his sight . . .
Craven heart—I wonder why
Lingering alone am I?

They were men of valiant breed,
Fit and fearless in the fight,
Who in every thought and deed
Burned the flame of life too bright.
Cowards, live while heroes die . . .
They have gone and—here am I.

*   *   *

Dumb Swede

WITH barbwire hooch they filled him full,
Till he was drunker than all hell,
And then they peddled him the bull
About a claim they had to sell.
A thousand bucks they made him pay,
Knowing that he had nothing more,
And when he begged it back next day,
And wept!—they kicked him from the door.

They reckoned they were mighty slick,
Them two tinhorns from Idaho;
That poor dumb Swede could swing a pick,
But that was all he'd ever know.
So sitting in a poker game,
They lost the price for which they sold

To that bonehead a poor dud claim
That didn't have a speck of gold.

My story's true as gospel creed
Of these bright boys from Idaho;
They made a sucker of that Swede
And laughed to see the poor boob go,
And work like nigger on his ground,
Bucked by the courage of despair . . .
Till lo! A rich pay-streak he found,
That made him twice a millionaire.

So two smart Alecs, mighty sick,
Begged jobs at fifteen bucks a day.
Then said the Swede: "Give each a pick
And let them sweat to make their pay."
And though he don't know what it means,
Folks call that Swede "magnanimous"
—But picking nuggets big as beans,
You oughta' hear them fellers cuss!

*   *   *

My Bear

I never killed a bear because
I always thought them critters was
               So kindo' cute;
Though round my shack they often came,
I'd raise my rifle and take aim,
               But couldn't shoot.
Yet there was one full six-feet tall
Who came each night and gobbled all
               The grub in sight;

On my pet garden truck he'd feast,
Until I thought I must at least
                    Give him a fright.

I put some corn mush in a pan;
He lapped it swiftly down and ran
                    With bruin glee;
A second day I did the same,
Again with eagerness he came
                    To gulp and flee.
The third day I mixed up a cross
Of mustard and tobacco sauce,
                    And ginger too,
Well spiced with pepper of cayenne,
Topped it with treacled mush, and then
                    Set out the brew.

He was a huge and husky chap;
I saw him shamble to the trap,
                    The dawn was dim.
He squatted down on his behind,
And through the cheese-cloth window-blind
                    I peeked at him.
I never saw a bear so glad;
A look of joy seraphic had
                    His visage brown;
He slavered, and without suspish-
—Ion hugged that horrid dish,
                    And swilled it down.

Just for a moment he was still,
Then he erupted loud and shrill
                    With frantic yell;
The picket fence he tried to vault;
He turned a double somersault,
                    And ran like hell.

I saw him leap into the lake,
As if a thirst of fire to slake,
                    And thresh up foam;
And then he sped along the shore,
And beat his breast with raucous roar,
                    And made for home.
I guess he told the folks back there
My homestead was taboo for bear,
                    For since that day,
Although my pumpkins star the ground,
No other bear has come around,
Nor trace of bruin have I found,
                    —Well, let me pray!

*   *   *

Mike

MY lead dog Mike was like a bear;
I reckon he was grizzly bred,
For when he reared up in the air
He over-topped me by a head.
He'd cuff me with his hefty paws,
Jest like a puppy actin' cute,
And I would swear: by Gosh! he was
The world's most mighty malemute.

But oh the grub that dog could eat!
Yet he was never belly-tight;
It almost broke me buying meat
To satisfy his appetite,
Then came a change I wondered at:
Returning when the dawn was dim,

He seemed mysteriously fat,
And scorned the bones I'd saved for him.

My shack was near the hospital,
Wherein there laboured Nurse Louise,
Who was to me a little pal
I planned in every way to please.
As books and sweets for her I bought,
My mug she seemed to kindo' like;
But Mike—he loved her quite a lot,
And she was very fond of Mike.

Strolling with her as moonlight gleamed,
I saw a strand of cotton trail
From Mike, the which unseemly seemed
To have its source behind his tail.
I trod on it with chagrin grim,
And with a kick his absence urged;
But as he ran, from out of him
Such yards and yards of lint emerged.

And then on me the truth did dawn
Beyond the shadow of a doubt:
That poor dam dog was gorged upon
The poultices Louise threw out. . . .
So "love my dog love me," I thought,
And seized the moment to propose . . .
Mike's dead, but in our garden lot
He's manure for a big dog-rose.

Black Moran

THE mule-skinner was Bill Jerome, the passengers were
     three;
Two tinhorns from the dives of Nome, and Father Tim
     McGee.
And as for sunny Southland bound, through weary woods
     they sped,
The solitude that ringed them round was silent as the dead.

Then where the trail crooked crazily, the frost-rimed horses
     reared,
And from behind a fallen tree a grim galoot appeared;
He wore a parki white as snow, a mask as black as soot,
And carelesslike weaved to and fro a gun as if to shoot.

"Stick up yer mitts an' freeze 'em there!" his raucous voice
          outrang,
And shaving them by just a hair a blazing rod went bang.
The sleigh jerked to a sharp stand-still : "Okay," drawled
     Bill Jerome,
"Could be, this guy who aims to kill is Black Moran from
     Nome."

"You lousy crooks," the bandit cried; "You're slickly heeled,
     I know;
Come, make it snappy, dump outside your booty in the
     snow."
The gambling pair went putty pale; they crimped as if with
     cold,
     And heaved upon the icy trail two hefty pokes of gold.

Then softly stepping from the sleigh came Father Tim
    McGee,
And speaking in his gentle way: "Accept my Cross," said he.
"For other treasure have I none, their guilty gold to swell . . .
Please take this crucifix, my son, and may it serve you well."

The bandit whispered in his ear: "Jeez-crize, you got me
    wrong.
I wouldn't rob you Father dear—to your *Church* I belong."
Then swiftly striding to the sleigh he dumped the gold back
    in,
And hollered: "On your knees and pray, you lousy sons of
    sin!"

"Praise God," said Father Tim McGee, "he made you
    restitution,
And if he ever kneels to me I'll give him absolution."
"I'll have you guys to understand," said Driver Bill Jerome,
"The squarest gunman in the land is Black Moran from
    Nome."

*   *   *

The Test

SOMETIMES a bit of rhyme I see
    In magazine or book
That makes such fond appeal to me
    Its flaws I overlook;
It may be just a simple lay,
    Yet humanly so pat,
That when I've scanned it twice I say:
    "I wish I'd written that."

But when I read some classic ode
   Of gods, and mighty men
To finish it I have to goad
   My patience now and then.
Although to thrill to it I try,
   Its organ note goes flat,
And honestly I cannot sigh:
   "I wish I'd written that."

Some poems lift aloft the mind,
   Some whisper to the heart;
Unto the last I'm more inclined,
   Though innocent of art.
Some verses get beneath my skin—
   Like *Casey at the Bat*,
Or *Jim Bloodso* or *Gunga Din*—
   Why didn't I write that?

These bards have got the edge on me,
   I've missed the lyric bus;
My rhymes and metres, I agree,
   Are sadly obvious.
My balladeering lays I rue,
   I'm just a copy-cat. . . .
Goldarn that devil, Dan McGrew—
   Oh why did I write that?

*   *   *

Death of a Croaker

YOU'VE heard of Montreal Maree,
   That rose of scented sin;
But are you hep to Doc' McGee
   Whose lubricant was gin?
The poor old Doc' has gone, I fear,
   To dry and dusty doom;
Yet why does Maree shed a tear
   So frequent on his tomb?

I'll tell you. It was in the whirl
   Around our Christmas tree,
Outshining every glamour girl
   Was Montreal Maree;
And of the rowdy bunch of us
   Who round her feet did flock,
None was half so assiduous
   And ardent as the Doc'.

Then Maree mounted on the stage
   To do her special show,
Her Floradora dance, the rage
   In circles of Sourdough.
And as the boys stood up and cheered
   Them shapely limbs to see,
The gayest of the gang who peered
   Was gallant Doc' McGee.

Then suddenly she paused to show
   A needle and some thread:
"Can any of you smarties sew?
   I've split my tights," she said.
A hundred answered to her call:
   "We surely can," cried we;
But most vociferous of all
   Was grey-haired Doc' McGee.

I heard the warning of Maree;
   I saw the frenzied rush.
Alas! Too late—poor Doc' McGee
   Was trampled in the crush.
Aye, when we dragged him to the light
   That gay old guy was dead;
Yet lo! His dauntless hand held tight
   A needle and some thread.

*   *   *

Bide-a-wee

YOU'VE heard, may be, of Maw McGee
   Who from Old Reekie came;
A lorn and lonely widder she,
   And sorry for the same;
Who put her scanty savings in
   A tiny shop for tea,
In Lucky Strike, that bed of sin,
   And called it Bide-a-wee.

The which is Scotch for Rest-A-While,
   But somehow no one did,

And poor Maw with a sickly smile
   Her woe and worry hid.
   Her hand-made scones and cookies were
   Forever growing stale,
For sourdoughs vinously aver
     Tea's splendid for the trail.

Then one day Montreal Maree,
   In gaily passing by
Saw silver-haired old Maw McGee
   Partaking of a cry.
So bold she breezed into the shop:
   "I like your joint," says she;
"And every afternoon I'll stop
   To have a cup of tea."

Right there she tuckered in with toast
   And orange-pecoe brew;
Of shortbread that was Scotland's boast
   She bought a pound or two.
Then to the dance-hall dolls she spoke:
   "I sink zere ees no doubt
Zat poor ol' leddy she go broke:
   We gotta help her out."

And so next day 'twas joy to see
   Them babies bargin' in,
And Maw was busy as a bee
   Amid a merry din.
And then the hooch-hounds lent their aid;
   Said they: "It's jest like home."
Why, even spoonin' marmalade
   Was Black Moran from Nome.

The Nugget Bar was lonesome-like
   From four to five each day,

And wondering was One-eyed Mike
   What kept the boys away.
Says he: "Where are them sons o' guns?
   I'll stroll the street to see."
When lo! he found them buying buns
   In jam-packed Bide-a-Wee.

The boys looked sheepish, I'll allow,
   As One-eyed Mike strolled in,
To see him kiss Maw on the brow
   And greet her with a grin.
"Why, bless you, dear, give me a pot,
   And make it strong," says he;
"Since Mother died I've quite forgot
   The taste of home-made tea."

So in the Camp of Lucky Strike
   Maw sure has made the grade,
And patronized by One-eyed Mike
   She plies a pretty trade.
To all the girls a mother's part
   She plays but oh how she
Is grateful for the golden heart
   Of Montreal Maree!

       *   *   *

Violet De Vere

YOU'VE heard of Violet de Vere, strip-teaser of renown
Whose sitting-base out-faired the face of any girl in town;
Well, she was hauled before the Bench for breachin' of the
   Peace,

Which signifies araisin' Cain, an' beatin' up the police.
So there she stood before the Court of ruddy Judge McGraw,
Whom folks called Old Necessity, because he knew no law.
Aye, crackin' in a silken gown, an' sheddin' of a tear,
Ashine wi' gold an' precious stones sat Violet de Vere.

Old Judge McGraw looked dourly down an' stroked his silver
    beard.
Says he: "Although the Sheriff's bruised, the lady should be
    heared.
What can you say in your defence? We'll give you a square
    deal."
"I jest forget," said Violet. "Maybe it was my heel.
I always want to kick the gong when I am feelin' gay;
It's most unfortunate, I guess, his face was in the way."
Then scratchin' of his snowy pow the Judge looked down
    severe,
Where bright wi' paint like plaster saint sat Violet de Vere.

Says he: "I'm going to impose a twenty dollar fine."
Says Violet: "Your Honour, to your judgement I resign.
I realize I should not my agility reveal:
Next time I'll kick the Sheriff with my toe and not my heel.
I'm grateful to the Court because I'm not put in the clink;
There's twenty plunks to pay my fine,—but now I come to
    think:
Judge, darlin', you've been owin' me five bucks for near a
    year:
Take fifteen,—there! We'll call it square," said Violet de
Vere.

The Twins of Lucky Strike

I'VE sung of Violet de Vere, that slinky, minky dame,
Of Gertie of the Diamond Tooth, and Touch-the-Button
    Nell,
And Maye Lamore,—at eighty-four I oughta blush wi' shame
That in my wild and woolly youth I knew them ladies well.
And Klondike Kit, and Gumboot Sue, and many I've forgot;
They had their faults, as I recall, the same as you and me;
But come to take them all in all, the daisy of the lot,
The glamour queen of dance-hall dames was Montreal
    Maree.

And yet her heart was bigger than a barn, the boys would
    say;
Always the first to help the weak, and so with words of woe,
She put me wise that Lipstick Lou was in the family way:
"An' who ze baby's fazzaire ees, only ze bon Dieu know."
Then on a black and bitter night passed on poor Lipstick
    Lou;
And by her bedside, midwife wise wi' tears aflowin' free,
Aholdin' out the newly born,—an' by gosh there was *two*:
"Helas! I am zere mossaire now," said Montreal Maree.

Said One-eyed Mike : "In Lucky Strike we've never yet had
    twins,"
As darin' inundation he held one upon each knee.
"Say, boys, ain't they a purty sight, as like's a pair o' pins—
We gotta hold a christinin' wi' Father Tim McGee."

"I aim to be their Godpa," bellowed Black Moran from
    Nome.
The guy wot don't love childer is a blasted S.O.B.:
So long as I can tote a gun them kids won't lack a home."
"I sink zey creep into my heart," said Montreal Maree.

'Twas hectic in the Nugget Bar, the hooch was flowin' free,
An' Lousetown Liz was singin' of how someone done her
    wrong,
Wi' sixty seeded sourdoughs all ahollerin' their glee,
When One-eyed Mike uprose an' called suspension of the
    song.
Says he: "Aloodin' to them twins, their age in months is two,
An' I propose wi' Christmas close, we offer them a tree.
'Twill sure be mighty pleasin' to the ghost o' Lipstick
    Lou..."
"Zen you will be ze Père Noël," said Montreal Maree.

The dance hall of the Nugget Bar erupted joy an' light,
An' set upon the stage them twins was elegant to see,
Like angel cherubs in their robes of pure baptismal white,
Abaskin' in the sunny smile o' Father Tim McGee.
Then on the bar stood Santa Claus, says he: "We'll form a
    Trust,
So all you sourdoughs heft your pokes an' hang 'em on the
    Tree.
To give them kids a chance in life we'll raise enough or bust!"
"For zem I pray ze Lord to bless," said Montreal Maree.

You never saw a Christmas Tree so swell as that, I vow,
Wi' sixty sweaty sourdoughs ringin' round them infants two;
Their solid pokes o' virgin gold aweighin' down each
    bough,
All singin' *Christ Is Risen*, for the soul o' Lipstick Lou.
"Lo! Death is a deliverer, the purger of our sins,
And Motherhood leads up to God," said Father Tim McGee.

Then all the Ladies of the Line bent down to kiss them twins,
Clasped to the breast, Madonna-like, of Montreal Maree.

Sure 'tis the love of childer makes for savin' of the soul,
And in Maternity the hope of humankind we see;
So though she wears no halo, headin' out for Heaven's goal,
Awheelin' of a double pram—bless Montreal Maree!